Praise for *Savi*

No one has seen their face with innocence and wonder. We bear bias fueled by industries of shame, and we are told we need something other than what we see to be loved. Aimee uses words as a mirror to see ourselves as God sees us in the gaze of his delight. This brilliant, compelling, and transformative book is a vision of what it will be like to be fully captured by the face of God.

—Dan B. Allender, PhD, professor of counseling psychology and founding president, The Seattle School of Theology and Psychology

Aimee Byrd is a treasure! In this age of spiritual disillusionment and abuse, she shows us how to fight through betrayal and hold on to Christ. But just as significantly, she gets vulnerable in this beautiful work, reminding us that we can never truly know God until we can face the truth about ourselves. And as we look Aimee full in the face, it's that much easier to see our own faces too—and long for the day when we all may see him, barefaced, unmasked, face-to-face.

—Sheila Wray Gregoire, founder of BareMarriage.com, and coauthor of *The Great Sex Rescue*

In Aimee's beautiful and personal new book *Saving Face*, we're invited into the wrestling ring—Aimee wrestling with God and with a Savior she knows so personally and intimately, wrestling with her image in the mirror and the good self she projects out into the world, wrestling with many different ways of doing church and with challenging and often overlooked texts of Scripture, wrestling with every weary and worn out version of herself. But what we're honored to see is her deep longing: to know and be known by God, to know and be known authentically in her relationships, to live with faithfulness and integrity. This book is a profound gift that will invite you into this holy wrestling as well.

—Chuck DeGroat, professor of pastoral care, executive director of the clinical counseling program, Western Theological Seminary, Michigan, author of *When Narcissism Goes to Church*

It takes a special kind of courage to face ourselves and see what truly is instead of what we've pretended to be or had to be or others believe us to be. Aimee Byrd has that courage, and *Saving Face* is the result of this deeply personal and spiritual work. One never gets the sense that this is a finished journey for her, but instead now, at midlife, she is truly making peace with the ongoing work of a storied life and the ways we are continually shaped and formed until we meet Christ face-to-face. A beautiful and tender book.

—Lore Ferguson Wilbert, author of *The Understory*,
A Curious Faith, and more

Aimee Byrd's *Saving Face* invites us to stop the charades and step away from the fake lives we often settle for. This book is for anyone who needs a reminder that God's realness is the only anchor strong enough to help us face our regrets, tell our secrets, and find the courage to live honestly again. In an age marked by mental health struggles and a generation longing for healing from the church, Byrd's words are a balm—pointing us back to the beauty of forgiveness, the sacredness of inconveniences, and the freedom of being fully seen. It left me feeling both challenged and deeply loved. I can't recommend it enough.

—Michelle Reyes, PhD, professor of cultural engagement at Wheaton College, author of the award-winning book *Becoming All Things*

What a gift this book is to those who have been hurt in and by the church, those who long for a place to be seen and known.

Out of her own painful story, Aimee Byrd invites us to join her in seeing what was always there: our true face. Beckoning the broken, welcoming the wounded, Byrd vulnerably models the good, hard work necessary for our true face to be restored in face-to-face communion with our Redeemer and with one another.

—Chris Davis, senior pastor of Groveton Baptist Church, author of *Bright Hope for Tomorrow: How Anticipating Jesus' Return Gives Strength for Today*

SAVING FACE

SAVING FACE

Finding My Self,
God, and One Another
Outside a Defaced Church

Aimee
Byrd

ZONDERVAN
REFLECTIVE

ZONDERVAN REFLECTIVE

Saving Face
Copyright © 2025 by Aimee Byrd

Published in Grand Rapids, Michigan, by Zondervan. Zondervan is a registered trademark of The Zondervan Corporation, L.L.C., a wholly owned subsidiary of HarperCollins Christian Publishing, Inc.

Requests for information should be addressed to customercare@harpercollins.com.

Zondervan titles may be purchased in bulk for educational, business, fundraising, or sales promotional use. For information, please email SpecialMarkets@Zondervan.com.

ISBN 978-0-310-16762-4 (audio)

Library of Congress Cataloging-in-Publication Data

Names: Byrd, Aimee, 1975- author.
Title: Saving face : finding my self, God, and one another outside a defaced church / Aimee Byrd.
Description: Grand Rapids, Michigan : Zondervan Reflective, 2025.
Identifiers: LCCN 2024038438 (print) | LCCN 2024038439 (ebook) | ISBN 9780310167600 (paperback) | ISBN 9780310167617 (ebook)
Subjects: LCSH: Jesus Christ--Face--Meditations. | Face--Religious aspects--Christianity--Meditations. | BISAC: RELIGION / Christian Ministry / Discipleship | RELIGION / Christian Living / Social Issues
Classification: LCC BT590.P45 B97 2025 (print) | LCC BT590.P45 (ebook) | DDC 231.7/6--dc23/eng/20241016
LC record available at https://lccn.loc.gov/2024038438
LC ebook record available at https://lccn.loc.gov/2024038439

Published in association with the literary agent Don Gates @THE GATES GROUP

Cover design and illustration: Wayne Brezinka
Interior design: Sara Colley

Printed in the United States of America

24 25 26 27 28 LBC 5 4 3 2 1

*To Blaine Rinehart and Margie Stemple,
the first faces that gazed into mine and showed
me I'm worth delighting in. Over and over.
Thank you for your faces, which are
helping me develop my own.*

CONTENTS

Part Three: The Blessed Face

Part Four: The Naked Face

Part Five: The Maturing Face

Preface

A FACE THAT FITS

We are all looking for a face. It's the first thing we do when we are born into this world. We look for a face looking at us, delighting in us.

We are all looking for our own face. That's a big part of these other faces, really. We come out asking, *Who am I? Who loves me? Why do I matter?* So we need to be seen. The first mirror we see is the face of another human. In the other's face we find our own.

We are all looking for God's face. This is the blessing: to see God's face, to see God's face looking at our face, to see God's face delighting in our face. Then we will know who we are. Then we will know we are loved. Then we will feel in our bones how we matter.

Our faces prove we were made for relationships in community. Our faces provoke a sense of meaning that calls us to hold one another responsible.[1] Our faces summon our humanness. They show our nakedness, our need, our truth. Can you do that? Can you look into the nakedness of another human face?[2] Can you reveal your own face before another so that you may learn the truth of who you are? Can we find our faces? Can we find God's face?

Looking into the nakedness of another's face is how we learn about who we are, the meaning of life, and therefore who God is. He shows up in the faces of others.

But we are busy trying to hide our faces, mask them, conform them to the face we think is acceptable—clamoring to discover what that is. We are, in a sense, terrified of our own faces, frightened to discover who we really are and, even more, to reveal who we really are to others. We are stuck in the hustle, and therefore we are only looking at the outside of things. The outside of our face and the outside of the face of the other. We have an unspoken agreement: I'll accept your mask if you accept mine. Ironically, it can be described with the idiom *saving face*.

It doesn't work though. Our longings are too deep. Too true. Too powerful. We need to dig them out of ourselves. We need one another's faces to excavate and nourish them. It turns out that pain, fear, and shame are working hard to strangle and malnourish our longings that need to be blessed. They trick us into believing that we cannot share our secrets, even with ourselves. They attack at the corners of our broken pieces, where beauty does its best work in the mending and creating. We need one another to listen and look. We need to be awakened to spring because the last of the winter snow is melting. God is calling us. And, amazingly, he wants to see our face and hear our voice (Song 2:14).

What is it about the face? What do we mean when we talk about God's face? Or our own? Why can it be so difficult to look someone in the eye? Especially a suffering someone? To hold that gaze? What is revealed? How do we find Christ in the faces of others? How do we find our own faces?

We all long for faces that fit. For faces worth saving. And we need one another's faces to call out our own. Looking into others' faces reveals a greater mystery. *Saving Face* is a reflection on the divine face and the meaning we get from the faces of others as we are trying to find our own. Our personhood will be consummated as we together make it to that day before the face of God. I am inviting you into a combination of storied memory, journaling with God, interactions with the faces of others, and relooking at the Scriptures in light of it all. Will you enter with me into a different kind of reading?

Prelude

TILL WE HAVE FACES

She covered her face. It was her one weakness, her ugliness. She wore a veil, and that gave her power. Or so she believed. Over time, people forgot her ugliness. She became a mystery. Her intelligence and leadership impressed an image of its own, and the veil provided a mystery to cover herself.

But then she got the very thing she wanted: to voice her complaints against the gods—to their faces. In this retelling and reshaping of the myth of Cupid and Psyche, we enter the story through the voice of the beautiful Psyche's sister, Orual. She had been cataloging her complaints against the gods for her misfortune and the injustice she faced. She was born with the misfortune of being not only a girl but an ugly one. Her little sister was the beautiful one. And Orual loved her, protected her, and mothered her. We see this as Orual built her case against the gods, beginning with the death of her mother (Was it because she didn't give the king a son?) and the cruelty of her father, the King of Glome. Orual rose above her looks, her loss, and the way she was treated. She was respectful to her tutor-slave, gaining both friendship and an education. She kept her love for the married soldier Bardia secret from him. She was always rising above the loss, becoming queen of Glome, sacrificing herself for her loyalty to her people. And in all of this, her undying love for Psyche motivated her. This was the way she saw it. This was the way she told it.

She wrote of the injustice when their father, the king, agreed with the priest that Psyche must be sacrificed to the gods to reverse the curse on Glome. Even worse, Psyche accepted this sacrifice as her fate. Orual would never forgive the gods for taking Psyche from her. Orual gave and gave, picturing herself more righteous than the gods. *She* knew love. *She* knew sacrifice. *She* knew beauty. *She* knew justice. And she was all alone. At the end of her life, Orual had a vision. This was her moment. She stood before the gods with everything she had documented in her book.

She stood naked before them. No veil. Barefaced. When she was told to read her complaint before the court—a moment she had been preparing for her whole life—her book felt different. Smaller. The pages in it seemed different, maybe even childish. Her carefully documented tragic memoir now appeared to be full of angry scribble. Orual mustered up her voice to read of her hatred. It poured out of her. She would rather have seen the brute gods of Glome devour her sister than what happened—they beckoned for her sister's love of a beautiful god. How could they? "We'd rather you drank their blood than stole their hearts. We'd rather they were ours and dead than yours and made immortal."[1] They dared to give her sister eyes to see their glory! Well, Orual refused to look. This was theft. Psyche belonged to her! What's worse is Psyche was happy there! Not Orual. She would have been happier to see her sister devoured by the beast than blissfully married to a god. On and on, she complained.

Eventually, the judge cut her off, saying "Enough." That's when she realized she was reading the same thing over and over, from beginning to end and back to the beginning. Her voice had not been recognizable to her, and yet she became certain that this was "at last" her "real voice."[2] There she stood in silence. Then the judge asked her if her complaint had been answered. And she said yes. She explains to the reader:

> The complaint was the answer. To have heard myself making it was to be answered. Lightly men talk of saying what they mean. Often when he was teaching me to write in Greek the Fox would say, "Child, to say the very thing you really mean, the whole of it, nothing more or nothing less or other than what you really mean; that's the whole art and joy of words." A glib saying. When the time comes to you at which you will be forced at last to utter the speech which has lain at the center of your soul for years, which you have, all that time, idiot-like, been saying over and over, you'll not talk about the joy of words. I saw well why the gods do not speak to us openly, nor let us answer. Till that word can be dug out of us, why should they hear the babble that we think we mean? How can they meet us face to face till we have faces?[3]

Now she saw the truth. Orual was wrong about love. It wasn't something to consume or to manage. It wasn't measured out by fractions. It wasn't manipulated by sacrifice or emotion. It doesn't cage or control. She had her answer.

"I know now, Lord, why you utter no answer. You are yourself the answer. Before your face questions die away."[4]

This is the story of my favorite novel, C. S. Lewis's *Till We Have Faces*. It so brilliantly reveals human struggle to unearth the truth about ourselves, about who we are, what we're made of, what we love, and most importantly who loves us. Before the divine face, the veil falls off, and we get to look in the mirror that Christ holds up for us. Then we see. Along the way, we get a few cracks at looking at ourselves in the mirror by looking at the faces of others. But for the most part, the story we tell ourselves often isn't close enough to reality. It's veiled. Orual was telling herself about her sacrificial love for her sister, for the married soldier Bardia, and her people. But it was the other way around. She was emotionally manipulating them. They were the ones sacrificing for her counterfeit notions of love. She was consuming them. It took a lifetime, the loss of what she fought fiercely to keep, and coming before the gods in order to hear her own voice, consider her own thoughts, and find true meaning, beauty, and love. What do the different faces we interact with reveal about us, about how we see God's love for us, and about how we love others?

I first read Lewis's novel in my early twenties. I wish I could say that I soaked up its powerful message in a way that put me on the fast track to maturity. That did not happen. That's not the way it happens. But it stuck with me. Back then, I did make a connection. Now on the downside of my forties, I finally reread the novel I've been claiming as my favorite for the last twenty-five years. And I returned to this connection. I wrote a bit about it in my last book,[5] but I want to think more deeply and really look at my life in light of *Till We Have Faces*.

In part, the book seems to be a commentary on 2 Corinthians 3:7–18. Paul is contrasting the ministry of the law of Moses with the ministry of the Spirit. The ministry of the law of Moses brought death in its condemnation, but it was still glorious. So much so, that Moses had to veil his face after the time he spent with God in receiving it, as God's glory radiated from it more than the Israelites could bear. It showed righteousness. With how much more glory does the enduring ministry of the Spirit, who *brings* righteousness, overflow? Paul explains that a veil remains draped over those with hardened hearts under the old covenant. That veil can only be removed by Christ: "Now the Lord is the Spirit, and where the Spirit of the Lord is, there is freedom. We all, with unveiled faces, are looking as in a mirror at the glory of the Lord and are being transformed into the same image from glory to glory; this is from the Lord who is the Spirit" (2 Cor. 3:17–18).

The ugliness of Orual's face symbolizes her pursuit of her own righteousness. This is what happens when our hearts are hardened. When we think the law of Moses is attainable. But we are only deceiving ourselves. And it sucks the life out of people. Our striving for a persona of righteousness is the love we take. We try to keep this revised edition of our goodness in our hands and in our hearts, but it turns black. We can't see that we are manipulating those who love us in order to serve our own fears and give us what we think we need. We deceive ourselves into thinking we're not asking for a lot. We don't need much. But the ugliness of it all is covered up by our veil. We can't bear to look at ourselves, so we direct our eyes elsewhere—to the virtues of our personified self.

But look at the freedom we get in God's love: "Now the Lord is the Spirit, and where the Spirit of the Lord is, there is freedom." Many pastors are too afraid to preach this message. The grace in it is too extravagant. What will people do if we send them off with this message? We are free from condemnation. We are *given* holiness so we can walk in it. We are *given* the eyes to see so the veil can be removed. We are *given* beauty as we reflect Christ.

What happens when we look at each other unveiled? It's like looking in a mirror at the glory of the Lord as we are being transformed into the same image and reflecting our unique angle of the picture. This is just too much, isn't it? This is what we want deep down. But our hope is being dug out of us as we look at our fears and false faces. We want the veil ripped off, and we want to see and reflect this glory. Christ in me; Christ in you. We want faces. We want to delight in one another's faces as we delight in the Lord together.

It's funny how you can get all the way into your forties or fifties before you let some truths out. Like memories and their impact on your whole life, what they mean, or what you really want. And it's just a glimpse, an undeveloped truth. My friends and I are getting better at this. My husband, Matt, and I are doing work here, and it's glorious. Maybe it takes this long because first you have to build a love strong enough to hold it. What a gift it is to be able to hold one another's stories, empathize with one another's wounds, begin to be more curious about why we react the way we do, help plow new neural pathways for self-reflection—to find our faces in one another. It makes me think about how much more complex and rich confession, repentance, and forgiveness is in the Christian life. It is so much more than the transactional functionality we present it as. Soul work is holistic. And it brings us to joy and beauty.

Finding our faces is a continual exercise. It is attunement to life. It's a hunt for reality and a communing in it. Rowan Williams tells us that this is where God happens:

> In this light, what is an honest "spiritual life"? Perhaps we should say that it is one in which the taste for truth, rather than sincerity, has become inescapable. We don't know what we will be, what face God will show to us in the mirror he holds up for us on the last day, but we can continue to question our own (and other people's) strange preference for the heavy burden of self-justification, self-creation, and weep for our reluctance to become persons and to be transfigured by the personal communion opened for us by Jesus.[6]

So we are developing our taste for truth. In doing so, I found myself questioning what truth even is. I used to think truth was a doctrinal matter, that truth was in certainty. It was objective and dehumanized. I'm learning that I was only looking at the outside of things. We have to be made ready for reality, for truth. As God is preparing us for the ultimate blessing of seeing his face in Christ, he gives us this lifetime to help one another uncover our faces and develop our taste for truth.

This life is where we live *Till We Have Faces*.

But *now* is kind of funny. Time is both linear and circular. The *then* carries into the *now*. Yet our memories don't exactly know the difference. They shape us in how we process them, feel them, experience them, recall them, speak them before the faces of others, and hold them together. You will experience this in my writing. This book includes my journal entries—in which I'm often talking with God—from a time when I was striving to overcome disillusionment while still aching for a church. I was striving and searching, wrestling and wanting. Allowing myself to experience these emotions is like looking into that mirror Christ is holding up. Looking into that mirror has prompted me to seek his face in the faces of those he put into my life, as well as in the face of Aimee during that time. What would I tell them now? What would I tell her now? Doing this work develops my face.

And it has convinced me that the church needs to develop her face. Christ is preparing us for love. The contemplatives that went before us speak of this development. Clare of Assisi beckons a disciple with a call that beckons you and me today: "Place your mind before the mirror of eternity!"[7] This is Christ. And this is what we will be practicing, reader, *Till We Have Faces.*

Part One

THE REFLECTED FACE

One

LOOKING FOR MY FACE

S o this is what it's like to be ugly."
I said those words out loud. I was in the fourth or fifth grade when my best friend Kathy Derr—who is two years older than me—talked me into cutting my hair short with a rattail. It would be so cool! All the guys were showing off this new style. How punk rock would it be for a girl to do! And she was convinced that I had the face for it.

To be clear, getting my hair cut didn't mean going to a trained stylist in a nice salon. It meant going to my mom and begging her for a few days, wearing her down. Mom was the stylist. But not really. She held no license. At least she wasn't one of those cringy bangs or bowl cut mom-stylists. She had an artistic eye. With a little mousse—a fascinating new hair product at the time—maybe I could pull it off as if it were a paid-for look.

I wore it with confidence to school. Did someone say something to make me feel ugly? Not that sticks in my memory. There were probably a few shocked students, asking, "What did you do to your hair? Why?" I do remember my teacher, Ms. Geasey, telling me how cool it was. It felt like she was trying to boost my confidence. It worked. But my hairstyle wasn't how I imagined it. It was too short. My cowlicks were now nuisances. The rattail was too long. Rattail—the name alone should have given me the sense to know it isn't a thing of beauty. I should have said, "No, Kathy! I'm not doing it!" But I was a people pleaser. I continually chased the allure of being a trendsetter. No other girls ran out to get the look.

When I arrived at this realization, I was in my family's main-floor bathroom, sitting on the counter, looking in the mirror, talking to myself, facing the facts. I was in the same spot I would go to investigate my face on other occasions, as close as I could get to the mirror. From that vantage point, I was known to examine the underneath of my tongue or the inside of my eyelid. How fascinating! I wonder what it looks like inside my nostrils! I studied myself in wonder. What do I look like when I make this face? What do people mean when they tell me that I have an expressive face? What makes mine more expressive than others? What's my real smile, and what's my fake smile? Which one is better? I wonder what I'd look like without eyebrows. Widow's peaks are so cool; I wish everyone could have one . . .

And now I was ugly. I never really thought about being ugly before. Did Kathy know this was going to make me ugly? This hairstyle just did not fit Aimee. I'm someone different now. Someone put-on. Someone trying too hard. How can I be this version of Aimee—the one with a fad haircut that seemed to rebel against the feminine? I'm proud of how that little girl handled it. "Moving on, looks aren't everything.

Hair grows out. Hold your head high and make sure you don't run out of mousse." I cut off the rattail myself shortly thereafter. My friends didn't treat me any differently. By the sixth grade, I got it cut into a rockin' bob. At a real salon.

Why in the world did this memory stick with me? Maybe feeling ugly for the first time had an impact, but it doesn't haunt me. The memory is focused on the inquisitive little girl looking in the mirror, trying to figure out what she looked like, who she was, sitting as close to the mirror as she can, as she did sometimes to check in. That mirror so clearly gave a reflection but never quite the answers. She needed to know how others saw her. It is before the faces of those who cared about her, and even many who didn't, that she began to learn about herself. They beckoned the Aimee out of her. The good parts and the not-so-good parts.

We need more than mirrors. We need more than countless selfies to stare at. Those provide only one version of ourselves that we see through our own eyes. It's like hearing your recorded voice for the first time. The recorded voice doesn't sound anything like the voice you hear while you're speaking. Your own voice sounds foreign. Strange. That's when you realize that other people hear you differently.

In some ways, we are complete strangers to ourselves. We look in the mirror wondering who we really are and who we are becoming. Mirror, mirror on the wall . . . tell me something about myself!

That day, I was seeing a false ugliness. A beautiful little girl with a bad haircut is hardly experiencing real ugliness. That Aimee is gloriously innocent of the cruelty of real ugly. She only knew the superficial. And she had mirrors: the one in the bathroom, the face of Kathy, her classmates, her teacher, and her parents. She was looking and had places to be curious.

THE FIRST MIRROR

The first mirror is the face of another human.

We cannot see our own face. This metaphor points to a deeper level of seeing. We cannot know ourselves without other human beings—a whole lot of them. How strange it is that before the face of the other, in the very otherness of the other, we find our own strangeness in all its glory. Contemplating this gives a depth of meaning to the creation story and the very first person. With the creation of each animal, God was teaching Adam about his humanity and how it is not good with just one sole self, not even in paradise. In the woman's creation, Adam also learned that beholding the face of another requires sacrifice. A death of sorts. Death to his sole self.[1] Death for the new creation from his side. He came from the dirt and returned to the dirt, to a deep sleep, for the creation of woman, who is not from the dirt. "At last," he says when he first lays eyes on her. Now, before her face, he knows more of who he is. Her face summons his own to move toward her, for her. That's part of who he is. He is *for another*. He is *with another*. And he can't know himself in any other way.

And that's just it, isn't it? I can look into a mirror and get a sense of what I look like. I can try to peer into the reflection in my eyes and catch a glimpse of my soul, of who I am, and of my character. But I can't get to it. I don't just want to see myself; I want to see how other people see me. I want to see the me they draw out. That's how we learn about ourselves, the eyes of others bear witness to our personhood, our unique qualities, our glory. And they summon our truest face. Writer and poet Cole Arthur Riley says it like this:

> We need other people to see our own faces—to bear witness to their beauty and truth. God has made it so that I can never truly know myself apart from another person. I cannot trust myself to describe the curve of my nose because I've never seen it. I want someone to bear witness to my face, that we could behold the image of God in one another and believe it on one another's behalf.[2]

To look at my face, I have to gaze into your face. What I see in the mirror is one dimensional. I can't get to the side of it or behind it. I can't see my own back or the reality of the curve of my nose. And this inability extends to my insides—my character, my soul, my intellect, my sense of humor, and even my narrating self.[3]

Richard Rohr considers the faces of others as mirrors, even as we are seeking the divine face. He says that God was given a face in Jesus Christ. And he uses the faces of each other to beckon what the commandments alone can't: empathy and love. Christianity is more than a moral matter; it is a mystical one. Rohr suggests maybe this is why the public image of Christianity is tainted with so many "mean" Christians. We depend on our commandments for transformation, while bypassing the heart and soul. Commandments speak to our wills, but the mystical "authentic I-Thou encounter" gives us more of a picture than a measuring stick. To encounter a face delighting in our own speaks to our longings, "giving us the face we can't give to ourselves." These encounters are less measurable, but far more impactful to soften our hearts and beckon our souls to love. "It is 'the face of the other' that finally creates us and, I am sorry to say, also destroys us. It is the gaze that does us in! Now surely you see why a positive and loving God-image is absolutely necessary for creating happy and healthy people. Without it, we will continue to create lots of mean Christians who have no way out of their hall of negative mirrors."[4]

HALL OF NEGATIVE MIRRORS

I've been down a hall of negative mirrors. Or more like a maze of them. I've found the mean Christians. I've been one too.

Follow me for a moment on a creative journey. A young adult, stepping into this house of mirrors, seeking a path to a mature spiritual life, seeking guidance, teaching, and community. It is welcoming. Look in these mirrors to find your face and the halls open for travel. You're among peers. They've entered likewise to study their faces in the mirrors, looking for others in the reflections. Over there, you see some of the elders' faces light up, speaking the things of God. These are mysteries of which you want to learn more. If only you could get to them. If only they could see your face looking at theirs. Maybe then they would invite you in.

So you stumble about, banging into mirrors that you thought were openings. Everywhere you look, your own reflection seems to mock you. The people you encounter, who live behind the mirrors, won't give you directions to move forward. And your feet only remember backward. You find yourself shuffling around, trying to navigate without another embarrassing collision. The mirrors are like invisible fences.

You notice the stacks the elders are holding: the commandments of the house of mirrors. The elders are reading from them. And you mistake the commandments for a map. You abide. You're with your peers. Your steps become more confident now that you have the map; you find some narrow openings and are allowed to sit at the elder's feet. But if you open your mouth or show curiosity, they stuff additional commandments down your throat. You're choking and gasping for air. They don't notice that you can't breathe.

You look in their faces and see judgment, contempt, and cruelty. And you realize that you're not the disillusioned one. Your feet were right. You need to backtrack your steps and get out of there. You can barely see the light at the entrance. Can they see it too? Are they looking past the piles of documents? If only you can get them to look at your face, maybe they will see hope. Maybe they will walk past the commandments to see real goodness. Maybe they'll make it out of the dead ends of mirrored walls and see real faces. He is there! The Beautiful One! But they are pointing and accusing: *Wicked! Defector!* Now your feet are moving with a determined cadence out of this hall of negative mirrors.

That's my story of looking for belonging in the church, of looking for Christ's face and my own too. Rohr described it exactly; it was a hall of negative mirrors. Have you been in a fun house before? Why are they called that? They aren't fun at all. They are terrifying. But that's how it was. I entered full of wonder and joy, wanting spiritual formation and growth and community. And I was first met with smiles. I didn't realize how the mirrors were positioned. It took me so long to see that the people inside had separated the commandments and laws from the face of Christ. No, it's not a fun house at all. It's a house of disillusionment. And now I sit with the grief of what I thought I had. I sit with the trauma of being reviled by those appointed as Christ's undershepherds.

With the loss of those I thought would be lifetime friends. And this is still my journey: finding my own face and looking for Christ's face in the faces of others.

LOOKING FOR MIRRORS

I had to say it—to myself, on paper, and out loud. For three years I'd been carrying grief. Much joy and newness has been given in it. But only because there was so much death. Grief is important. It needs to be recognized, felt, expressed, and seen and held by others. And so I confessed on paper a gratefulness for the grief. For the agony that refused to let me stay numb. For the pain that woke me up to then die to faux blessings and false belonging and success and needing to give my kids the "right" path to the faith. I thought I was building something foundational for their faith, raising them in the "right" church with the "right" doctrines, making sure they looked and behaved the way that a Christian is supposed to. I had to confess to my failure and the sadness I carry for showing them such an incomplete picture of God and for being this far in life without something as basic as a church.

I had to die to the wealth I thought I'd fashioned in my spirit—the wealth of my persona of goodness. To wipe off the "everything's okay" smile and take up mourning. To recognize the other blessed, broken believers who mourn how disillusioned they were too.

I wrote it all down. Journaling has been a valuable part of the work I am doing not only to heal from church harm and disillusionment but also to reach the blessing: to see and experience Christ and to do so in the face of the people before me. So I journaled.

January 31, 2023

Today, sitting with the sadness that our family doesn't have a church home, that one cannot seem to be found, that as we search, I carry the shame of the labels "troublemaker," "resistor," "woman" into new spaces. How will I be seen? Will I be seen?

Today, sitting with the fear that accompanies the bravery of reaching out to another pastor to inquire about his church for our family. That's a scary thing for me to do right now. In the dysregulation of this vulnerability and all it conjures up from my history of not being safe in church. Opening up to someone in spiritual authority. Hoping they believe me.

But you know how God is. He's showing us signs of his love and guidance all the time. He wants us to do this work, exploring the reservoir of our souls so that we can empty out what doesn't belong. Like Orual, we want him to take the anguish. He wants us to listen to it. He shows me that sometimes in my reading. That's how I found this timely treasure from Walter Brueggemann: "The riddle and insight of biblical faith is the awareness that only anguish leads to life, only grieving leads to joy, and only embraced endings permit new beginnings."[5] Ah, yes! My soul needs that salve.

The poetry and lamentation of Jeremiah, Brueggemann says,[6] speaks prophetically into Israel's numbness and Jeremiah's anguish: "The alternative community knows it need not engage in deception. It can stand in solidarity with the dying, for those are the ones who hope. Jeremiah, faithful to Moses, understood what numb people will never know, that only grievers can experience their experiences and move on."[7] Grievers let go of the hustle, the false narrative, the numbing, the closing of the eyes, and the self-deception that we make our own blessing. In our agony, we are in need. In our agony, we see others in need. In our agony, we are given hope, and we feel.

Many have wondered over the short verse, "Jesus wept" (John 11:35). We sentimentalize it and carry it in our change purse, not allowing its weight to be felt.

But I want to look at his weeping face. What does it tell me? Here's what Brueggemann finds:

> But now I understand the depth of that verse. Jesus knew what we numb ones must always learn again: (a) that weeping must be real because endings are real; and (b) that weeping permits newness. His weeping permits the kingdom to come. Such weeping is a radical criticism, a fearful dismantling because it means the end of all machismo; weeping is something kings rarely do without losing their thrones. Yet the loss of thrones is precisely what is called for in radical criticism.[8]

Write this down, Aimee. Sit with it. Gaze upon Christ's weeping face.

I've seen the thrones and the numbness in my own faith community. I've experienced the agony of its machismo. The complete lack of imagination, wonder, and awe of what God is doing. The dehumanizing. Their faces are empty. I've had to die there, from there. With all its losses. Hope is born, maybe especially in the continual ache. But more needs to die of my own thrones.

Lord, thank you for grief. Thank you for this portal to imagine who you really are. How uncontrollable your love is. How out of our bounds it is. How generous and wise it is! The door to our imagination opens at these deaths, reveling in your freedom to create something new there. A whole new world within a world.

I imagine you now, your weeping face as a mirror. Is there anything more trustworthy than a weeping Savior who faced the dregs of darkness and the pit of agony to fill us with himself?

PAST, PRESENT, AND ETERNAL MIRRORS

My college Childhood Psychology professor asked us all to conjure up our earliest memory. I had never thought about that before. I felt a little silly when it popped in my head. We had to share them with the class. Mine was just a glimpse of a flashback. I must have been three because we were still in our town house. Grandma and Pap Pap arrived with a Sit 'n Spin toy for me. I remember spinning and spinning—the freedom and joy of it. I remember Grandma watching me with delight. And that's it.

That's all I had to share with the class. Apparently, our earliest memory speaks to our personality. And there is three-year-old Aimee, spinning away. At least I wasn't the guy who said his first memory was looking through the front window, watching his brother and dad play in the snow, feeling sad that he couldn't join them. I bet he has a lot of psychological work to do! I'm awful like that, making fun of others to feel better about myself. Clearly there is much work to be done for me too.

But I've come to love little, spinning Aimee. This brief flashback has rich layers to it. My grandparents brought me a gift and reveled in my joy. I responded with joy—the joy of receiving, being loved, of loving things, of my hands grabbing onto the wheel, legs wrapped around tightly, and turning my whole body over and over. I had the freedom to move, as well as the freedom to delight and be delighted in. That's a pretty great first memory.

It reminds me again of what Richard Rohr said: "We are mirrored not by concepts, but by faces delighting in us—giving us the face we can't give to ourselves. It is 'the face of the other' that finally creates us and, I am sorry to say, also destroys us. It is the gaze that does us in!"[1]

It's the gaze that does us in! A gaze has its own vocabulary. We learn more about ourselves from others' gazes than we do by their words. The right side of the brain reads faces, and the face-reading right side is the turbo side. Jim Wilder shares:

> It takes about 165 milliseconds (a sixth of a second) for a full round trip from one right brain to another right brain and back again. It will take our conscious mind 15 milliseconds longer to become aware that we have seen someone's face. By then, a second round is already underway. Through this fast-track "thinking," the minds of two people begin to synchronize. In a matter of seconds, they are using the same circuits, matching chemistry, experiencing similar energy levels, and sharing one experience.
>
> Right-to-right brain communication is rapid, authentic, and quite a bit faster than conscious thought can track. Consciously, we are too slow to fake our messages.[2]

The forty-three muscles on the face don't lie. We are quick to pick up that face that is delighting in us, as we are constantly looking for it. As we mind-match with others, or develop mutual mind through the process Wilder explained, we make a third thing: *us*. A type of me drawn out of you and you drawn out of me. We find each other and ourselves and even God. He shows up on our faces. These micro-encounters shape our knowledge of the divine face that we image.

My earliest memory is a flashback of a micro-encounter I had with my dear grandma. It's encoded in my explicit memory as a glimpse. But deep down, my implicit memory was already familiar with many earlier connections: Grandma and me sharing moments, making *us*. And God showed up in her delighting gaze. She mirrored his delight. The message was clear: *You are beloved. I delight in seeing your joy. I am happy to be with you. Spin, Aimee, spin!*

THE MIRROR OF ETERNITY

Place your mind before the mirror of eternity![3]

Clare of Assisi (1194–1253), one of the first followers of Francis of Assisi and founder of the Order of Poor Ladies for women in the Franciscan tradition, wrote the words above in a letter to Agnes of Prague. Clare picked up the same theme in a subsequent letter:

> *since he is the radiance of eternal glory*
> *is the brightness of eternal light and*
> *the mirror without blemish.*

Gaze upon that mirror each day . . .
     and continually study your face in it . . .

Indeed,
    in that mirror,
        blessed poverty,
            holy humility,
                and inexpressible charity shine forth
            as, with the grace of God,
                you will be able to contemplate
                    them throughout
                    the entire mirror.[4]

Jesus Christ is the mirror of God, the mirror of eternity. To look at him is to look at what is real. What do we see in the mirror? "The Son is the radiance of God's glory and the exact expression of his nature, sustaining all things by his powerful word" (Heb. 1:3). That line of Scripture always makes me pause in wonder. This is who we are called to look to: the radiance of God's glory! But more than that, he is a wonder to behold. His is a face we can only see by contemplation now, but we long to see him looking at our face when all is set right. By looking into his eternal face, we find poverty, humility, and charity. St. Clare was passionate about living a life of poverty, as for her this is how the life of contemplation thrived. Ascetic living is a challenge to our thinking today. At least, it is for me. I don't want to downplay her own focus on material poverty. It does make me think about how we loath poverty, fear it—but not only material poverty.

I never used to think of myself in the beatitudes. I would read it as Christ comforting the unfortunate with the promise of what is to come. "Blessed are the poor in spirit, for the kingdom of heaven is theirs" (Matt. 5:3). Now I know in my body more of what it means to be poor in spirit. Your idea of security is stripped away. You experience a scarcity of sanctuary. When I felt that lack, I got a better look at the eternal mirror of the kingdom of heaven. We think we are living in the real now. We look to our work, our neighborhoods, our friendships, our church, our family, our healthy living, our quiet times, our networks. They assure us of our blessings. And gratitude for them is good and right. Experiencing disillusionment with the church and my friends helped me see that my "rich" picture was disillusioned already. The blessedness of poverty is being able to see what's real and finding true riches. Seeing the blessedness of poverty in the eternal mirror is seeing that we are filled with Christ. He is the gift. He did not withhold himself when he took on flesh. His body is given for us, offered to us over and over again in holy sacrament to nourish us with himself. We need to look into this mirror and study our faces in it. Who are we before the poverty and richness of Christ?

St. Clare writes to her sisters that they are a mirror to one another and to others, so that those who see Christ in their faces will also become a mirror and testimony of Christ and the love he has for his people.[5]

By looking at the eternal face, we find our own.

MEETING THE FACE OF ANOTHER PASTOR

My family's been searching for a church for a year and a half, in need of spiritual nourishment, beauty, goodness, love. We've been through a dearth of spiritual vitality, of hospitality, of substance. We've seen all the gimmicks and the striving. We've barely met Christ in these places built for him. And so, here we go again. Matt and I getting ready to meet with another pastor for coffee to find out about his nondenominational church plant. These conversations take emotional work.

I arrive vulnerable. Did he Google me after our email exchange? I'm a few clicks away from a bad first impression before he even sees my face. Will he think I really am what these other church leaders call me? A troublemaker? Jezebel? Or worse, will he be like others who offer empathy as I confide in him but then act awkward around me in church as if the trauma I hold is like a bomb that might go off at any minute? As if I'm walking around with a bunch of triggers? Or maybe he will think I'm just too much.

February 3, 2023

This ache inside of me. I will bless it. Even though it turned into anxiety that woke me up at 4:00 a.m. That ache that longs to be in a real church helps me to get back up again. Strengthen my weak knees. To be vulnerable even when it triggers the trauma.

But it also helps me to shed some of the false self that I thought was real. The fear and the anxiety that coddles false self, though! Wanting to be protected by its shield. Wanting others to think it's me. Shielding the fears of giving too much of myself only to be rejected. Fears that my being a woman diminishes the value of my voice. And that big fear: that I'm too much. A troublemaker. Help me properly repent of this and lament where we are, Lord.

So we go . . . to Starbucks. It doesn't appear that the pastor has Googled me. As we talk, I think about how a year ago I wouldn't even have considered this church. And yet I learn we have some similarities. We hold in common the disillusionment from spiritual abuse and the deconstructing of so much we held dear before. We hold in common discoveries we've made—the wonder of neuroscience and its implications on spiritual formation, and the pursuit of beauty, goodness, and truth that Christ is. My heart leaps over these things.

But is this pastor deconstructing too much? Will he lead by what he confesses about Christ? As we connected over how our thinking has changed and how love is primary in the church, the actual details of how this church worships chinked away at my new, growing hope. They don't sing yet because they don't have the talent to lead them. (Do we wait for talent or just start singing?) They have no liturgy. No shared confession time. The service is just a sermon. And on the first Sunday of the month, breakfast and a Q and A. What does he believe, and what does he preach? I asked if he subscribed to the Nicene Creed. He responded that he saw it as a good baseline, but he didn't want to impose that on others. What does he mean by that? I understand the hospitality to promote belonging and am more convinced that belonging comes before belief. But are we going to be worshiping the same God? Will there ever be a liturgy, Bible reading, congregational praying, singing? I'm encouraged by his desire to invest in others' potential to lead—women too!—and his humility in gleaning from the perspective of others not like him. This is what I want and what I am afraid of. Is he deconstructing too much? Will he have a solid foundation on Christ in which we can rest?

He doesn't see you in the Old Testament. I mean, he says he does, but he doesn't. Am I really going to take the task of being a missionary here?

The Reflected Face

To invite others to behold the beauty and typology in the story? He's missing the juice! Will he want to put the brakes on me wanting to point it out? Will I just be another troublemaker yet again?

Can we call this church? Can we call it worship? Am I deconstructed all the way down to "For where two or three are gathered together in my name, I am there among them" (Matt. 18:20)?

Then there's the sexuality thing. He didn't say "affirming," but that this church doesn't divide over the issue. I don't want to divide. I want to honor everyone. I also want to promote goodness and holiness. How can a church do all this? Where do I stand on this? And doesn't a church need to say what their position is, one way or the other?

Will all this ambiguity be good or bad for my young adult "kids" to see? They are almost out of the nest, and we are running out of chances to expose and immerse them in goodness.

Should we at least take a look at what is going on here? Where else is left to go? What does God want to show us?

We are so disillusioned with church. And yet I have this ache for her. For your love for her. For us.

This church is so many of the things I used to warn about in my writing. But that certainty I had before was a farce. It missed the mark.

I feel like we've come full circle. Starting our marriage with little knowledge of God in a loving community. Curiosity. Loving the mystics, but as I "gained knowledge" feeling shame for that. Like I needed the right theology to protect me. So I pursued it with full vigor because I wanted to know you truly. I wanted to do this faith thing right as an adult. Be the right wife. The right mom. Launch good, Christian offspring. And now we are going to be curious about a church that embraces the uncertainty. Can we really be guided by love? What is love, then?

What would you say to me here, Lord?

I'm imagining you saying, "You know my voice. Listen for my voice. You will recognize me and what I am making."

I've lost trust in myself. But not in you. You nourish me even without the church I ache for. You work outside your temple. You have moved into our very souls. Dwelling there. Help me to be Christ for others and to look for you in them as well. Keep me focused. The face of this pastor called out my poverty. In that mirror I am reminded of your blessed poverty, holy humility, and inexpressible charity. Blessed are those who listen to their anguish. Thank you for the ache, Lord. For seeing me, comforting me, and bringing me to its satisfaction.

Three

WHAT IS HELD INSIDE

Now, let's conjure up what is held inside my second memory. I couldn't have been older than four. My neighbor and I were playing, and we went into his house. He said something about their TV being broken. He wanted to go back outside. But I wanted to stay inside and see it—the broken television. We went outside, but my mind was racing while we were playing. If his TV was broken, maybe all our favorite characters were escaping from it. Maybe they were in his house! I wanted to go check. This would be amazing!

As I recall this, I wonder what our second memory says about our personality. Spinning Aimee has begun to contemplate things and has developed quite an imagination.

What if the world is like this broken television of my imagination? I look at the sky a lot. When I was younger, I would wonder in awe when the clouds would open up to the sun, revealing what could only be shekinah glory. I'd imagine that this beam of light was a rip in heaven that God allowed to reveal a glimpse of his glory and that of the angels with him. Was it a portal that we could enter? Jacob's ladder?

Maybe those unplanned moments when we make a knowing connection with someone are like that. We share a moment from another dimension. The characters within us sneak out from their containers. We take a peek. But it leaves such an impression.

MIRROR NEURONS

It's often an ache that beckons us to look outside of ourselves and into the faces of others. We are constantly looking for integration, as our minds know this is the path to wholeness, to "finding our face." Our mind-matching, turbocharged, curious right brains are busy working on this for us. Additionally, neuroscientists have discovered that we have mirror neurons at work, constantly mind-mapping, anticipating, and mimicking the actions, emotional energy, and even sometimes the physiological state of those around us.[1] Have you ever felt the need to scratch your face when your conversation partner does? Have you found yourself with your legs crossed the same way or getting thirsty when you see someone take a drink? How about the strange contagious yawn phenomenon? Mirror neurons! Everyone hates a copycat, but this is what we are wired to do! Maybe this is why Scripture warns us to be careful about who we spend our time with: "Do not be misled: 'Bad company corrupts good character'" (1 Cor. 15:33 NIV). (If only we can figure out how good or bad our company is. Or the company of our own thoughts.)

Mirroring is part of our survival. Dan Siegel, a pioneer

in the field of interpersonal neurobiology, points out, "At the most complex level, mirror neurons help us to understand the nature of culture and how our shared behaviors bind us together, mind to mind."[2] All of our senses work together, mind-mapping with others to anticipate, resonate, empathize, and connect. In perceiving others and our environment, we are able to perceive ourselves more clearly. It's mind-bending to think about. Within this resonating with another, we discover our own beautiful differentiation as well. We must be in tune to our own bodies and minds to read another's well. Siegel explains that we understand how another person is feeling because we know how that feels in our own bodies. We know what it feels like to be sad, so we can empathize with another who is sad. We feel it with them in this way. We connect with laughter in the room, as our own bodies resonate with this glee. Being in tune with these bodily sensations also helps us to differentiate and "discern who is 'me' and who is 'you.'"[3] The more attuned we are to the state of our own bodies, the more empathetic we can be, and the more we can mature in self-awareness and realize the ways we are influenced.

"Finding our face" is really about integration, about becoming whole in our longings, emotions, faith, knowledge, behavior, and relationships. Isn't this what we mean when we talk about our true selves? The masks we wear, the stuff we bury down deep inside of us, the status, people, and lifestyles we chase for the version of ourselves that we think we are—it's all disintegrating. We become rigid or chaotic in trying to hold all these notions together and stave off the parts of us that we don't want to see or feel. We think we are after self-autonomy, which is a faux freedom. Freedom isn't self-autonomy. This faux freedom requires power over others. It takes. True freedom gives. It is a recognition of ourselves and one another as gift. True freedom leads to the harmony and reciprocity that promotes integration.

Becoming more aware of mirror neurons helps us. Much of our perception and the resonances created by this system happen without our conscious effort. But by attuning to this interpersonal networking of our minds and bodies, we "can gain new clarity about who we are, what shapes us, and how we can in turn shape our lives."[4] We are continuously holding up a mirror, helping one another find our faces.

BLACK MIRROR

Charlie Brooker, creator of the popular sci-fi Netflix show *Black Mirror*, magnified my four-year-old imagination of what's behind the TV screen. The show's title refers to what we see when we look at our devices when they are not on. The technology inside our cell phones, tablets, and other screens often draws out darker parts of us—our longing for approval, artificial connections, insatiable desires to consume, compare, criticize, and worse. Just staring at the black screen before it lights up can be like a reflection of what is going on in our psyche and souls. What will we find? Worlds are held in these small screens.

There's a world where mirror neurons are usually turned off and faces are often obscured. In this world, we are usually looking oh so hard, oh so desperately, but the messages are jumbled. Everything seems unclear or even deranged. In this dystopia, your fears and anxieties are personified. Sometimes you get a chance to face them and see that they aren't as terrifying as you thought. Other times you're faced with fears you've stuffed down so well in the real world that you hardly recognize them. In this world, you can be startled by your own emotions, desires, and behaviors. The day version of yourself wouldn't think of such things. But this is the night world, where we live in our dreams. The dreams we conjure hold up a black mirror to illuminate the dark. They help us process and compartmentalize what our conscious selves cannot hold—that is, the pieces we cannot make sense of but that will not dissolve into the ether. They linger and wait for us to fall asleep.

Most dreams function like a filing cabinet, organizing implicit memories in ways we will hopefully be able to manage better. No need to consciously address them. We don't remember most of them anyway. Some dreams powerfully provoke our senses and emotions in ways that stick with us in the morning and throughout the next day. Sometimes I record these. I'm not promoting dream interpretation as authoritative science to live by. (Should I say that sentence twice?) But this is a chapter about what's held inside as I'm introducing the face as a mirror, and that is how I see our dreams helping us. They hold up a mirror. It is a black mirror of sorts, so it can be confusing and certainly disrupting. But we can be curious. What is disturbing or disruptive about it? How did it make me feel? What senses did it evoke? Why might that be?

Dreams seem to be only able to be recalled in pieces, which makes sense with the way time works—or doesn't—in them. Time isn't linear, anyway. Scenes change abruptly. There's a lot of symbolism. Even though they are not dreams, I think the Song of Songs and the book of Revelation function in a similar way. There's so much to glean. But we also see that dreams can be teachers in Scripture. The Bible records twenty-one dreams, predominately in the Old Testament. While some of the biblical dreams are laden with symbolism, God explicitly communicates with people in others. Many of us long for that explicit communication, although I don't know that we would welcome what God has to say. We might not be ready for it. Sometimes the black-mirror dream world aligns with reality better than our conscious perceptions.

I enjoy going back and reading some of the dreams that I've recorded. Here's one from when I was still thick in the aftershock of leaving my old church and denomination, still facing harassment, gaslighting, and insecurity about what spaces I would be accepted in. It was less than a month before I preached for the first time, which was something I was keeping on the down-low to avoid further judgment and harassment (yeah, that didn't work). I often end my dream recordings with a snippet of the current events that may have led to the dream.

February 27, 2022

Valerie, Rachel, and I agreed to live for a while in some house because we were in danger or something. Kind of like a witness protection. Our stay there was taking way longer than we were told; I even got to go home to visit but had to come back. The men who were supposed to be helping us were getting more covert, whispery. I found out they were planning to sell my house but still weren't telling me. It was all part of the operation. Then I had enough and said, "Hell, no," and "I'm out, I'm going home." Everyone was making dinner when I said this. And behaving weirdly—like they all knew that I couldn't leave, that they wouldn't let me.

There was another scene in the dream where they (who are the "they"??) told me they figured out who was behind all this. They then showed me a pile of vipers. It was the weirdest feeling to see them: a combination of seeing evil itself and also seeing they weren't even real people ... there was something pathetic in that.

Ugh, and in real life, last night I found out I'm being harassed again by men from my old denomination and others for my upcoming preaching engagement at Covenant.

WHAT'S INSIDE THE BLACK MIRROR?

Reading it now, a year and a half later, is enlightening. It is easier to see what my mind was processing from this perspective. Valerie and Rachel are long distance friends of mine, fellow writers who also were being harassed by these church leaders. A pastor in my old denomination even wrote a series of articles about how we were soldiers in the feminist army, for which I was the general. Which is absurd because Valerie is much more worthy of the title than me. And I mean that in all the best ways. I now see how loaded every single line of my dream memory is.

In my dream, the process was "taking much longer." Yes! The whole process I endured of "the proper church channels" to try and seek help and accountability was so slow and convoluted. That was a black mirror of its own!

"I even got to go home to visit but had to come back." At this point in my story, I landed on my feet and found new friends who appreciated my work and invited me to collaborate. And yet, frequently, waves of men from the spaces I left tried to pull me back in to conform to their infected, abusive system.

"Witness protection" might refer to all the men who stepped up to help me. Here, let us handle this, Aimee. We will protect you. The very act of accepting their help took away my voice. I had no agency. I was hidden away from the places where decisions were made. My life in the church and beyond was put on hold. But no worries, *they*'ll take care of this very important work.

"The men who were supposed to be helping us were getting more covert, whispery. I found out they were planning to sell my house but still weren't telling me. It was all part of the operation." All the decisions were made behind closed doors. There were layers of betrayal from those who were supposed to be my friends and spiritual leaders. I was also finding out that some who ostensibly were "helping" me were saying unsavory things about me to others. This is the most devastating part of disillusionment.

"Then I had enough and said, 'hell no,' and, 'I'm out, I'm going home.'" Now the dream is getting redemptive. I have found that my agency has been there all along. I saw what was happening and attuned myself to the signals. My voice came out.

"Everyone was making dinner when I said this. And behaving weirdly—like they all knew that I couldn't leave, that they wouldn't let me." Ah, not so fast, Aimee. The benevolence, the protection—it's kayfabe. ("In professional wrestling, kayfabe is the portrayal of staged events within the industry as 'real' or 'true,' specifically the portrayal of competition, rivalries, and relationships between participants as being genuine and not staged. The term kayfabe has evolved to also become a code word of sorts for maintaining this 'reality' within the direct or indirect presence of the general public."[5]) We keep your enemies close to us. We need them and they need us to uphold our fragile sense of selves and power. Everyone is making dinner; it's business as usual. Faux safety and belonging are gathered around the table.

"There was another scene in the dream where they (who are the "they"??) told me they figured out who was behind all this. They then showed me a pile of vipers. It was the weirdest feeling to see them: a combination of seeing evil itself and also seeing they weren't even real people . . . there was something pathetic in that." Thank goodness for the choppy scene shifts in dreams. This next vision resolves the conflict of the "Hotel California" *you can never leave* lie. It's the Scooby Doo unveiling of the bad guys. This is the scene that viscerally stuck to me still in the morning. How I felt both the horror of beholding true evil and their impotence. A pile of vipers can be a terrifying thing to find, but they have no face. They aren't human.

My dream helped me process these fears, wounds, and emotions. It helped me name some of the perceptions that I was suppressing. It helped me have agency and to see how evil is dehumanizing. It's beast-like. Real healing happened because of it. Not every dream is a gift like this. We certainly cannot will such dreams into existence. But we can spend time looking in that black mirror when we receive a curiously disruptive dream.

BLACK MIRROR CHURCH?

My family decided to give that nondenominational church a visit on the Sunday after meeting the pastor for coffee. But it brought more confusion. More people were there than the under fifty expected. By the time we arrived ten minutes early, they were bringing out extra round tables and chairs.

I dug sitting around tables. We tried to find one in the back, but it was really the front. The only person at that table so far was a crunchy-looking woman with a tat sleeve on her arm. I thought, *Cool, there's a story there.* When I got a closer look, I realized she was transgender. Her name was Avery. *Whew, God, you are just getting a real laugh at me, aren't you?* Not because I don't want to sit next to her—just in how I was confronted by the paradox of my convictions: What is goodness for her, and how do I honor her? She's timid, not really looking up from her cup of coffee until we greeted her and asked her name. Her voice is subdued so that we had to lean in to hear it. I got a great cup of pour-over coffee while others were grabbing breakfast for their first Sunday of the month discussion. During the worship service. That *is* the service.

The people were diverse. They looked genuinely happy to be there. And they seemed curious. We haven't seen curious people like this in church for a long time. They were friendly. We had good conversations with the people around our tables and with others. My son and daughter were engaged in the conversations. I loved how the tables helped us see the faces of people in church. I wondered if I've ever been to a church where a trans woman like Avery could join us.

The talk began. It had a Q and A format where the questions were already collected and fielded. The respondents included the pastor, another young man who cofounded the church plant, and Amber, the spiritual director. The pastor introduced Amber by saying she was about to get her PhD. Very intriguing. In some ways, I loved how the questions were answered—a lot of the freedom in belonging, the neuroscience, and humility that are green church flags for me. But I wanted more Scripture, more prayerfulness, more good news—an invitation to behold Christ and walk in the newness of his world. I wished there was singing. I knew that statistically a few singers and musicians must be hiding in this bunch. I began to wonder whether the leaders hadn't taken the next step because they only knew the "professional," pretend-rock-stars mentality of previous churches, didn't want that anymore, and didn't know what else to do. That's the most generous excuse I can muster. I also wonder if they don't want to sing the words of certainty about God in worship music. Confession leads to doxology. There was no doxology.

My family needs something to hold fast to. I need to know if the leadership is going to have confessional requirements for the teachers. I would be happy with the Nicene Creed. This isn't asking a lot; it's the bare minimum of orthodox Christianity.

I approach Amber on our way out and ask her what her dissertation is on. She is very excited to talk to me and responds that it is about storied communion. Right up my alley. I give her my contact info and ask to get together soon. She texted me a couple hours later. Turns out she lives very close to me. Whoa! We decide to meet that Thursday for coffee.

February 6, 2023

I just don't know. The kids seem curious. Matt and I share the same concerns. And mixed feelings. I'm so confused now that I don't even know if this is church.

But more and more, I am seeing how ungodly the church culture we were in is. How they used such certainty and elitism to coddle hate, indifference, hierarchy, tribes. I see my old friends and colleagues posting hate on top of hate, conspiracy, and fearmongering on social media. I want no part of that. Christ is not there.

And I'm left to wonder about how my old church and denomination and this experience are so very different. Like two black mirrors helping me face myself. What is held inside each one? What do I see when I look at them? What do I see when the lights aren't on and the performance of worship is set aside? Whose faces can I make out better? Where are the messages jumbled? And what fears of my own am I being faced with in each?

This church search is going to take more patience. I don't know if I have any more. But you are so patient with us, Lord. We are striving and grasping and flailing. Hold us fast. Help us notice the glimpses of you. And pause, that we may be still and see you. Listen for you. In church. On social media. At home. In Avery.

WHAT DOES THE MIRROR REVEAL?

There is a strange section in Scripture. That's an understatement. There are *many* strange sections in Scripture! Some of them are very disturbing. But most of them make me pause to try and figure out the mystery. One strange passage in the Old Testament involves women ministering at the entrance of the tabernacle. And it involves mirrors. Having spent almost my whole life in churches where only men could minister, lead, preach, and handle the Word of God during worship, this strange verse is even stranger. And I do not recall ever hearing a thing about it in church. Granted, the story is located in a long, detailed section of Exodus about building the tabernacle. In my Bible, this one verse has its own heading for Bezalel's work, which is sandwiched between detailed sections about him making the altar of burnt offering and the courtyard:

> He made the bronze basin and its stand from the bronze
> mirrors of the women who served at the entrance to the
> tent of meeting. (Ex. 38:8)

What a curious line. Simply enough, the verse is about the making of the bronze basin, the laver for the tabernacle. But it has some peculiarities. This is one of those verses that is supposed to make us stumble a bit.

Why didn't Bezalel use the bronze that was part of the general collection of supplies, of which they had more than they needed (5,310 lb.)? Why is it notable that the basin was made by melting down metal from mirrors given by specific people (Ex. 35:4–5; 36:4–5; 38:29)?

How are these women serving at the tent of meeting when the tabernacle hasn't been built yet?

Women? Serving? Tent of Meeting? What are these women doing so close to the priestly action?

I've done some theological work on the typology of women, revealing how women symbolically picture the collective bride of Christ/mother/Zion.[1] Maybe this verse standing on its own is a type-scene of sorts, outlining a picture that is filled out more in the pages of the canon of Scripture. When a text is full of so much mystery, it's good to ask about the symbolism and take a second look.

What about these mirrors? Mirrors reflect but cannot make one beautiful. We could discuss all kinds of interpretive possibilities, such as how these women got their mirrors from the Egyptian women or the interesting Jewish midrash about how the women used the mirrors to defy Pharaoh, seduce their husbands, and birth the whole host of Israel from their wombs. Rabbi Rachel Adelman notes how "the mirror, both as object and symbol, became ritually metonymic for woman and femininity in some Ancient Near Eastern sources."[2] It's interesting to think about how such a feminine symbol is selected to make the cultic laver. All that is good stuff.

But I want to get back to the basics. Mirrors reflect, they show what's on the outside. What if these women have found their Groom? And he beautifies from the inside. Instead of the dim reflection of their own faces from polished bronze or copper, they want to reflect the radiance of God—like Moses did! And they did this in their ministry at the entrance to the tent.

There is plenty of debate over what this vocational description of ministering means,[3] but here it is, in all its vagueness, recorded in the Word of God for us to see. Another place in Scripture where we see a reference to these women is in 1 Samuel 2:22, where we learn that Eli's sons were "sleeping with the women who served at the entrance to the tent of meeting," which was a despising of the Lord (2:30). Here, the women are abused. And yet we see that these women were ministering again. The Exodus text reads as an anachronism—a big word meaning it is imposed from another period of time onto our text—given that the tabernacle had not yet been completed. We see that this ministering function is retrojected into the text for us to notice. It's proleptic! That's another great word that we don't use very much. We call it proleptic when Scripture gives us pictures of the future represented as if they are already so. For this text, it is as if the women in Exodus are already ministering at the entrance of the New Jerusalem in all its glory. In this way, both of our texts on these women at the tent of meeting are activated in reading it.

That makes me want to read the two texts together and ask what Aaron and his sons saw when they came to that basin. Let's think a little about this bronze basin made from the women's mirrors. Basins or bowls are often used as images of fullness, and when they are associated with worship, they "connote the presence of God and his holiness."[4] We see in Exodus 30 that this basin is anointed with oil, consecrated as holy. Aaron and his sons must cleanse their hands and feet from this basin whenever they enter the tent of meeting. What do they see in this mirrored bronze? They see their own depravity and need for washing. But the holy mirror laver should reflect the Lord to them before they burn an offering for him.

And this is where I am seeing more of a type-scene before us. It is a basin made from the women's mirrors. It's like a womb of sorts, a baptismal font, wellspring, habitation of liveliness, as this laver reflects Christ back to them. It activates another verse for me as well.

We have much of this typico-symbolic representation in the story of the woman at the well. She also has a vessel for water. She's also unclean. The scene is dripping with betrothal literary narrative. Back in the day, wells were the place to go to find a bride: Rebekah, Rachel, Zipporah—all well-women.[5] "Jesus answered, 'If you knew the gift of God, and who is saying to you, "Give me a drink," you would ask him, and he would give you living water'" (John 4:10). She looks at Jesus, and he reflects her very self back at her. He knows about her many husbands. He is drawing it out of her, so she can learn that although she is like that woman passed from husband to husband in Deuteronomy 24:1–4—such that her own body, which is to represent sacred space, has been defiled, and she has no real husband now—Jesus is the faithful husband and high priest. He gives her dignity. Do you see the habitation of liveliness here? This defiled woman is learning that she is to be "a garden spring, a well of flowing water" (Song 4:15). All these cultic, or priestly, connotations lead her to ask about true worship and the hoped-for Messiah. "Jesus told her, 'I, the one speaking to you, am he'" (John 4:26).

So she goes and calls out: "'Come, see a man who told me everything I ever did. Could this be the Messiah?' They left the town and made their way to him" (4:29–30). The tent of meeting just enlarged—the Samaritans got in!

Women are at the entrance of the tent of meeting for a reason. They *are* mirrors of the radiance and glory of Christ's bride. They point to the wellspring of life! They testify to the coming Messiah, even when they are abused. How vile it was for Eli's sons to defile them! The women and their mirror-crafted bronze basin at the entrance of the tabernacle ministered by their very embodiment and personhood. *They* are proleptic, as if the total Christ—Christ united to his people—is already realized. Their very presence, alongside the mirrored bronze of the wash basin, signifies the radiance of God's glory! It's a mirror that really can tell us something. As priestly mediators, Aaron's sons were to wash up in the basin while contemplating the eternal face of the Lord God and his people—the Messiah and his bride. Instead of provoking a holy longing for the day when our union is consummated, finding the Lord's poverty to emulate the giving of themselves, humility, and charity, they took and defiled. The eternal mirror held before them revealed how they despised the Lord.

These texts serve as reverberations of the bride in Revelation and of the New Jerusalem coming down out of heaven from God. She joins her voice to the Spirit's, beckoning her brothers and sisters to "come."

Both the Spirit and the bride say, "Come!" Let anyone who hears, say, "Come!" Let the one who is thirsty come. Let the one who desires take the water of life freely. (Rev. 22:17)

He who testifies about these things says, "Yes, I am coming soon."

Amen! Come, Lord Jesus! (Rev. 22:20)

> The LORD gave the command;
> > a great company of women brought the good
> > news. (Ps. 68:11)

Christ loved the church and gave himself for her to make her holy, cleansing her with the washing of water by the word. (Eph. 5:25–26)

Part Two

THE
FRACTURED
FACE

DISRUPTIONS TO OUR SENSE OF SELF

In the third grade, I memorized a little ditty that was part of our story time. It was quite the earworm. Actually, that's what the story was about: the whole town could not stop singing this song once they heard it. It was nonsense, yet it made so much sense. Since my friends were impressed, I thought maybe it would earn me some good-hearted approval from my teacher, Ms. Beachly. I have fond memories of how she summoned my creative and contemplative side with writing assignments such as "Write a story based on what you see in this picture." Ms. Beachly got a real kick out of my recitation of this silly ditty and sent me next door to Ms. Geasey's classroom to recite it for her. It really must be an earworm, as it's stuck with me even today:

> Sing hi-diddle-diddle,
> For a silly little vittle.
> Sing git-gat-gittle,

Got a hole in the middle.
Sing dough-de-dough-dough,
There's dough, you know.
There's not no nuts
In you-know-whats.
In a whole doughnut
There's a nice whole hole.
When you take a big bite,
Hold the whole hole tight.
    If a little bit bitten,
    Or a great bit bitten,
Any whole hole with a hole bitten in it,
Is a holey whole hole
And it JUST—PLAIN—ISN'T![1]

You see how fractured this is, don't you? A holey whole hole. A whole hole with holes. Something must be done about this. It just plain isn't. Holey holes that are no longer whole is the kind of nonsense that makes us smarter. Singing it does, anyway.

WHAT HAPPENED TO MY FACE?

All this time, I thought I had a face. Like Orual, I thought my face was there, even if veiled. I thought all my convictions scribbled in book margins were certain, righteous, important. I thought I could bring them before God and get a real nod of approval. Look at all my gold stars! How careful I was to get you right, God! To show others the way. To show my children. To belong with the people who kept you reverent.

In a whole doughnut
There's a nice whole hole.

We are so busy looking for faces that delight in us that we don't realize how we are hustling to construct a face we think others, including God, will delight in. That face isn't genuine. Sure, parts of it are genuine. Those are probably our best parts. But there comes a time in our lives when we are disrupted, when we realize there are many holes: in what we believe, in who we think we are, in the meaning we are searching for. And we find that our faces are fractured.

When you take a big bite,
Hold the whole hole tight.

Oh, yes, I was holding the whole hole tight! I didn't realize how fragile my whole sense of self and ideas of sanctification were. So I worked hard to build "The Good Me." If you look back on your life and pinpoint the disruptions to your sense of self, what would they be? Before going through the traumatic disruption in my former church and denomination, I didn't realize how much of my life was a response to the catastrophe of my parents' divorce. But this spiritual disturbance to the story I was telling myself revealed that for proper healing, I needed to do the work of coming to terms with my whole story *before* all this church drama happened.

When I was young, my parents sang together. Not professionally. Not formally. After dinner, dad would pull out his guitar and mom would start washing the dishes. What a moment. My dad, whom I later learned has stage fright, played and sang some of his favorite tunes: "Black Bird," "Teach Your Children," "Here Comes the Sun," "Jesus Is

Just Alright with Me," and "Black Water." I thought that was natural until I learned he didn't do that in front of other people. His voice is lovely. And mom harmonized so beautifully while she did the dishes. It was as if dad played and sang only to glorify her beautiful voice. He played for her to join in. I thought this was what family was about. This was the gift. This was the goal. This was what I wanted.

Until I was of age to do the dishes.

There wasn't any singing then. My memories change here. What were my parents doing after dinner now? Watching *Jeopardy!*? I know what I was doing—complaining. "Why don't we have a dishwasher?" "We do," they would reply. The joke being that I was the dishwasher. Nothing was beautiful about this. No one was in the kitchen. What was once like a symphony to my soul became utilitarian and isolating.

They stopped singing together.

In hindsight, I know there were a lot of factors: work, life, a new dishwasher-person. But mainly it was their own past trauma. I knew nothing about it at the time. Well, maybe a little. The crumbs were all there. None of our minds saw the crumbs.

> If a little bit bitten,
> Or a great bit bitten,
> Any whole hole with a hole bitten in it,
> Is a holey whole hole

THE GOOD ME

My parents' divorce was absurd to me. I had fifteen years benefiting from their love for one another and for their children. I had two creative, beautiful parents who loved Jesus, took us to church, and showed us beauty: in nature, in playfulness, in work, in art, in fitness. I had a great childhood. What happened?

The divorce revealed, in its own way, that we weren't really connected in church. We were Sunday attenders and servers, but not much else. No one helped us through the catastrophe. We just faded away.

I wanted to be faded for a while. The shame of it all. The disillusionment. The loss of place and security in family, church, self. What is real? "Absolute futility. Everything is futile" (Eccl. 1:2).

Have you ever cataloged the times that you've sensed God's presence? Felt him? Experienced him? In those moments, God's realness breaks into your existence, and therefore you too somehow feel more real? Usually for me, these moments occur during my encounters with beauty, whether in nature or in other people's faces. They happen during encounters with his Word and so powerfully in deep moments of anguish. As a little girl I always felt his comforting presence as I lay alone in my bed at night. We talked. But one time stands out. It changed the course of my life.

I was partying with my friends in college. Using the word *partying* is a way of making it vague. Maybe you are thinking of me around a bunch of drunken people at a frat house. I wasn't partying in that sense. *Tell the whole truth, Aimee.* I was tripping on LSD with about five people. Now you're not going to think that I was a good person who deserved to encounter God. And maybe you'll doubt that this experience was real, that it was just the drugs. All I can say is that it interrupted my psychedelic plans for the evening. And I encountered such gripping beauty, as God's realness contrasted with the fake authentic life I was living, that from that moment forward I've been driven to know him, love him, and become like him. He disoriented me in my disorientation.

So I stumbled about in my new work building The Good Me.

Fast-forward through almost ten years of chasing righteousness and offending others in the process. I caught my reflection in the master bathroom mirror and stopped cold. Just look at her. Look at me. I was in the third trimester with my third child, carrying a basket of dirty laundry, and downright exhausted. I looked at her, and that's when I realized what she was doing. I caught her eyes and, just for a micromoment, was able to read them. There was a hidden panic. Can I really do this? *Do what? Have three kids?* That's when it hit me. *This.*

Have exactly as many kids as my mom had, only do it better. Show her. *This is how you do it. This is how you stay.* This is what I needed to complete the broken cycle and mend it for the next generations.

That's what this was. The secret *this* that I was keeping from myself.

What an idiot!

I had to break it to the girl in the mirror feigning responsible motherhood. *No, you cannot. You are allowed to be exhausted. Stop this charade. You didn't come from where she came from. You can't really know. And you are running a fool's errand. Figure out you.*

Figuring myself out is taking a lot longer than I expected. But the faces of those three offspring, who are now young adults, are teaching me a lot.

That moment of clarity in facing my reflection softened me toward my mother, and so much healing has come from that. Staring back at The Good Me, the me that was going to be a better version than my mom, revealed a version of me I didn't like. And I softened toward myself as well. But The Good Me didn't die so quickly.

I couldn't simplify my parents' marriage unraveling and blame it solely on a lack of community at church. But I had the opportunity to give my kids a better connection in a better church. You know, one that educated us more about good theology. Superior theology. So for over twenty years, The Good Me put her energy into being in the right church, doing all the right things. We got connected and rooted our family in the body of believers. The *me* me was there too. I thought *me* me was fully in charge, longing to learn more about God, to experience his presence more in my life and in my relationships. I didn't realize how much The Good Me and the *me* me were competing with each other until church leaders in my own denomination questioned my goodness. Except it wasn't a question. It was an all-out character assassination based on all the writing I so carefully wove from the threads of our church's confessional standards. I used the very tools my denomination gave to construct an apologetic for the dignity of my sex as fellow disciples in the church. And all hell broke loose.

The absurdity of it all was palpable. The futility of me thinking I could reason with these pastors and church officers using our own church standards—heck, by using the standards of human decency. My naivety in thinking that, surely, if this is how these men think and behave, then they will be disqualified from their credentials to lead others spiritually with authority. How could I have thought that the teaching for church members and the protection offered to them was for the women too.

Once again, I was face-to-face with The Good Me. She was absurd. She was hiding in my virtues and wanted to come out swinging in defense. Economist and philosopher E. F. Schumacher observes that it's this kind of nonsense that makes us smarter: "When things are most contradictory, absurd, difficult, and frustrating, then, *just then*, life really makes sense: as mechanism provoking and almost forcing us to develop toward higher Levels of Being."[2]

> There's not no nuts
> In you-know-whats.

ON UNLEARNING

Why does God let us carry on so long with fractured faces? And will we receive the gift of him revealing this fracturing to us? I thought I had the face of a "good Christian woman." Sure, I knew I wasn't all good. I knew, and my theology made clear, that my heart and mind were depraved. I had conflicting desires and actions that only the indwelling Spirit of the triune God could transform, that only the body and blood of Jesus Christ resurrected and advocating at the right hand of the Father could atone for. But I thought I put myself in the places where this work was going to radiate through me to my children. I thought Matt and I gave our family a sense of belonging in the church, a community where we cared for one another's souls.

I built and I built with theological precision, service, and friendship. And I lived in a world full of invisible fences. Something wasn't right. In one of my earlier books encouraging women to grow in their knowledge of God, I quoted

Donald Macleod, saying, "I hope that while I still have much to learn, I don't have too much to un-learn."[3] That's a good hope. I didn't want to be that person. But unlearning is a continuous process in this life. Turns out, there is still much to unlearn. And I am grateful for that.

February 3, 2023

What misery it would be if we had to retain what we learn as certainty for our lifetimes! What a rigid way to live. Unlearning is a part of learning. And this gives us freedom and humility, then, to explore who we are, Lord, and your world with your people.

There is grief and shame in seeing how I clung to certainty. But you are so full of grace that it makes me excited at the same time. Your goodness is much more glorious than I thought it was, than I could even imagine before! This strange mix of emotions humbles me. And I'm afraid to use that word—humble—because it can be so performative. Pride loves to hide in that virtue. It's a humility that is in the threshold, beginning to see something for what it is, so that something loses its power over us. But in that turning, or in that crossing the threshold, there is a vulnerability to the new. What is it going to be? Can I handle it? Will I like it? Humility searches for trust, not certainty. Humility embraces unlearning to see the real. Please meet me at the threshold.

Isn't repentance also a form of unlearning? Dallas Willard paraphrases Jesus's words in Matthew 4:17 like this: "Rethink your life in light of the fact that the kingdom of heaven is now open to all."[4] Repentance is just that: rethinking, seeing what's real, turning toward it, shedding the counterfeit, and walking through the door. There's an unlearning involved.

Artist Makoto Fujimura proposes that repentance is provoked by an encounter with the beautiful.[5] Think about that! Beauty beckons us into the realm of goodness. There we find the reality of truth—not just truth's propositional statements but its *reality*. And we are free to deconstruct all the false striving we have done to find it and free to grieve that loss. Our grasping fingers find the strength to let go of the imitations.

What a gift unlearning is! We see that God is so much bigger and so much more abundant than our scarcity containers.

Learning with the finitude of our preresurrection bodies involves unlearning—and we have so much more to learn! Think about the way God designed the neuroplasticity of our brains so we can rewire new pathways of understanding. Consider how our minds depend on connections with other minds to learn about ourselves. In doing so, I get to unlearn and learn more about myself too.

Why is it so hard to say, "I was wrong"? Why do we struggle to admit that something is off in the story we are telling to ourselves?

The gift of unlearning frees us to take risks, to lead with love, to be curious and empathetic in light of the fact that the kingdom of heaven is open to all, and even to be known intimately by others and God. Unlearning can help us experience God. We can shed the things we think limit him and his love.

Thank you, Lord, that this middle-aged woman can be blessed and bless others with unlearning. Thank you that the truth of who you are transcends my own certainty. Help me to loosen my grip on things I need to unlearn. To see the beauty in the invitation. To stop covering up all my fractures with what isn't real. To trust in your terms instead of clinging to my own out of fear.

Sometimes it takes a disruption to help us see what we need to unlearn. What if our disruptions more closely attune us to look for what is beautiful? Wouldn't that help steer us? Wouldn't that make it easier to loosen our grasp on false realities? Disruptions to our sense of self are usually accompanied by open doors. We just might have trouble seeing them. As philosopher D. C. Schindler shares, "If beauty represents an *invitation* to the real, and goodness our *involvement* in it in freedom, truth is above all our *reception* of reality, on its terms. It is for this reason a living relationship, one with the capacity to transform."[6]

Six

A GOOD NAME

Our birthdays are only four days apart. I am the elder, but she is the wiser, the much more adventurous and creative. Jess has been my friend as far back as memories go. Same age, same church, same elementary, middle, and high schools. We spent long hours investigating the cornfield behind her backyard, making up stories with the treasures we found; making "slime" from all the soap, shampoo, and beauty products in her house, pouring it on her bushes to see what happened; devising disgusting pranks that no one fell for, such as making soap ice cubes out of our shared bath water. We grew up together sharing gossip, teenage dreams, and even experiencing our parents' divorces around the same time. Jess first, as she always was. We knew one another front, back, and inside out. So I thought.

Turns out I really didn't know myself. Those middle school years are brutal to one's sense of self. I was a bit timid, loved fashion, and was a late bloomer. With all the anxieties that stirred up, it felt pretty good when the more assertive new girl, who also loved fashion and was tiny like me, wanted to be besties. Over-the-top besties. She was a plotter, planning who we would talk to, what we were going to wear, when we were going to match outfits, which boys were important, who we would like, and who we wouldn't like. I went along with it.

Fully developed Jess was posing a problem to our relationship. Not really, but according to my new bestie, Jess had a list of troubling attributes that were cramping our style. And according to my new bestie, I needed to write Jess a letter telling her all the reasons I cannot be her friend anymore.

And I did it.

I don't understand those people who say they have no regrets in life. Why did I wear that ridiculous rainbow-explosion of a shirt on picture day, what was I thinking dating *that* guy, and *that* guy, and *that* guy, why didn't I listen and engage better in my history classes, why didn't I play a real sport instead of excel in cheerleading, why didn't I pay more interest and time in friendships with those who weren't as popular? And I haven't even gotten to the college years and beyond. So many regrets. But this one with Jess haunts me. How could I do this to my friend? I let a new bestie dictate the words as I wrote them down. We probably folded the letter into its own pretty envelope, as we did then, to obscure the cruelty inside it. We probably slipped it into her locker or some other cowardly delivery instead of a face-to-face handoff.

The pain I must have caused her haunts me still.

I don't know how long she let it sit. The heaviness on her, the arrogance of me. But my next memory, besides the continuous pit in my stomach, is Jess looking me in the eyes and saying, "This isn't you." She knew me. She gave me grace. She restored us. And she gave me freedom.

FOOL ME TWICE...

Fast-forward through many more glorious Jess memories to me being her maid of honor in her wedding. Had she not given me that grace in middle school, we would have missed out on so much. My redheaded, adventurous friend moved to the other side of the country when we turned eighteen. We never did live close by after that. And she moved around more in her new, married life. But for the next ten years, we kept in touch through letters and long-distance phone calls, gradually getting cell phones that still weren't equipped with the social media we have today. But I didn't know that Jess's marriage was falling apart until it was almost over. I heard some things that I did not verify with Jess—maintaining The Good Me face—and I couldn't believe Jess was going to let this happen after what we went through together with our own parents. We knew of the brokenness. The Good Me decided to write Jess a letter. What the hell is the matter with me, I do not know. The *me* me was quiet as a mouse and let The Good Me take over. I thought I was her. I had the audacity to use the words of the Puritan Samuel Rutherford to tell Jess how she was not being The Good Jess. I didn't say that, but that's what I said. It's all so humiliating to share—me humiliating her again. As an adult this time. No empathy. No curiosity. Convinced that her goodness and happiness was in "making it work." No idea what was really going on in her life. I was going to save her with this shaming letter.

She called me, letting me know some of these things. Pleading with me to see. But this time, she couldn't say, "This isn't you." The Good Aimee was fooling us all, strong in her convictions, certain she knew what was best for Jess. Our thirty-one-year-old selves were in two different dimensions. For the first time, we couldn't find each other.

Two of my deep life regrets are letters to Jess. But they are so revealing. Of my ugliness. My cruelty. For My Good Name.

Over time, when I saw it, she accepted my apology. We've mended some. But we are not the same Aimee and Jess. I put a deep fracture in the relationship. Who can blame her, after a second letter like that, for thinking I was just trying to fool her twice? For not trusting that the real Aimee isn't The Good Me? And The Good Me is cruel and destructive.

THE GRAVE BIOGRAPHY

There's memoir in Ecclesiastes. Of course it's in the book wrestling with everything under the sun being futile. Our philosophical, spiritual guide in Ecclesiastes seems to adapt an Egyptian literary form known as grave biography, which had been used for at least two thousand years. The name is self-explanatory. The deceased were remembered with writings on funerary monuments or the walls of their tomb. Our teacher in Ecclesiastes uses all three elements of a grave biography in his memoir—"a recitation of accomplishments, a collection of ethical maxims that had guided the deceased through an exemplary life, and exhortations to visitors to reflect on their own death and live accordingly"—but with a twist. As Ellen Davis points out, "Whereas the Egyptian grave biographies testified (truly or falsely) to successful lives, [our teacher] produces a poignant admission of failure."[1] I like this guy. While the Egyptians are pleading their case before the people and the gods of why they should be remembered on earth and welcomed into eternal bliss, our teacher tells us that God has given him a miserable task of futility as he pursues through wisdom all that is done under the sun (Eccl. 1:13–14).

In a sense, we are all writing our own grave biography. We want them to be spoken through weeping tears at our funerals. We labor to build our resumes of a good name. What is it? We often think we are pursuing virtues only to find we are constructing an imaginary self that is built on shadows. We cannot grasp the goodness because there is no substance, only a dark silhouette of virtue. I don't want to find myself standing in the shadows when I meet death.

What is my grave biography? If we ask this question from the wisdom gleaned in Ecclesiastes, we will think less about what good name we are trying to create and more about what our souls, like cisterns, have been holding inside all our lives. What is in there, and what did we gain? Who do we impact with it? What does it do to others? What is its eternal value?

When we begin to learn to do the work of looking into what our cisterns hold, we find our secrets. The ones we've been keeping from ourselves. And we begin to look at what we really think about God and are afraid he might do to or ask of us. When Paul encountered the risen Christ, he went blind for three days. And then scales fell from his eyes (Acts 9:1–19), including all those accomplishments he listed in his letter to the Philippians: "circumcised the eighth day, of the nation of Israel, of the tribe of Benjamin, a Hebrew born of Hebrews; regarding the law, a Pharisee; regarding zeal, persecuting the church; regarding the righteousness that is in the law, blameless" (Phil. 3:5–6). He built the good name, and it resulted in killing off God's people. We can safely say that he missed the juice. He missed Christ. Turns out Paul's cistern was dark, blind, and full of loathing. It was full of fear and scarcity. Until Christ held up the mirror.

If we are willing to tell our secrets and face our regrets, we can begin to learn what our cisterns hold. The futility is in letting them hide and fester, not realizing how they are working for the Egyptian grave biographies full of faux importance and not the memoir before the assembly of the "book of incongruities"[2] that is Ecclesiastes. The thing is, we are masters at hiding these secrets, even from ourselves. We can face our own incongruities and the incongruities of this world and lay them before God. Doing memory work is one way to get to our secrets. In it, we come face-to-face with ourselves and how we perceive our story. Interpersonal neurobiology is finding that our ability to make sense of our own stories and how they affect us determines our mental and emotional well-being and integration far more than the events themselves that happened in our past.[3] In learning to name what we were going through, name our fears, insecurities, different relational attachments with our loved ones, disappointments, and desires, we gain the empowerment of resilience in our narratives to remake and begin to love others more truly.

So why am I looking at these memories of Jess? They are fractures to my face. To my sense of self. To what kind of person I want to be, what kind of friend. And frankly, I miss her. I miss us. I hate what I did to her. I still carry the sadness and loss. Jess drew out a part of me that only she can. She holds so much of my history.

And why did I do it? The simple answer is that at the time I was valuing the wrong things: superficial belonging and popularity in middle school, and superficial righteousness in my thirties. That's getting somewhere, but it's deeper than that. Why did I value those things? *Go deeper, Aimee.* They were shielding my fears. In middle school, the fear was humiliation and invisibility. Middle school is so awkward. Full of mean, hormone-fueled prepubescents vying for place. I feared humiliation, so I humiliated my own friend in my place. I feared being invisible, so I erased my friend. That wasn't my intention, but it was my impact. Deep down, I was willing to sacrifice her.

Oh, the battle I am doing in my own heart and head right now. The incongruity with the story I've been telling myself all this time: I was the kind kid in middle school, not like the others. I stood up for the girl who smelled from peeing herself as everyone followed her around, making the noise, *psssssss.* Do you see my competing selves? I defended the disabled and the marginalized while cruelly erasing my best friend and listing all that was supposedly wrong with her.

As an adult I feared abandonment. Jess's divorce triggered that fear big-time. We went through those feelings of abandonment together as children without naming them. There we were, about ten years into our marriages, and she was going to repeat the cycle. I wore such the coat of self-righteousness not to face that fear. The cages that I put around my loved ones. *I* would not be *that. I* was so far from *that. That* was not going to happen to my family. How was anyone able to live with me then? I do not know. Jess sure couldn't. She needed a friend.

Reflecting on my accomplishments must include being able to uncover secrets and face them. Because I want to love better, truer, freer. Because these are my ethical maxims. Because this is what I value. Because death is letting our fears steer the wheel that leads us into futility. The fracture I caused speaks loudly to my soul—no longer to shame, but to resurrect and develop a face worth showing.

PUTTING THE GOOD NAME IN THE GRAVE WITH JESUS

I've named the ways I've been humiliated in the church; I need to name the ways I've humiliated others. I recognized earlier how that fear of abandonment was affecting my marriage, and I had to decide whether I was going to continue to let it form the kind of wife Matt came home to each day. It was scary to give him my vulnerability and to not be suspicious. I gave him the key to walk out of some of the caging I made in our marriage. But I didn't see how it affected my friendship. How it turned into self-righteousness. And I never thought I'd see my fear of abandonment surface in church.

Walking away from my Presbyterian denomination was a descent from the mountaintop of the certainty I relished in my faith. It's where I thought my good name was solid. In my mind, the Presbyterian church was the last place that would abandon me. But many leaders and friends did. And boy did I need them. I thought I did, anyway. It's a scary thing, though, when the ones that you rely on to be there with Christ's love don't have it to offer you.

We knew it would be difficult to find another church. We needed to heal. We didn't know when we would be able to build trust again. Before visiting the church that we weren't sure was a church, we'd been attending a nondenominational one that ministered to those who were deconstructing or suspicious of the church. I appreciated that the pastor and his wife were sensitive to spiritual abuse and had been through it themselves for standing up against child sexual abuse and cover-up. We liked that there was diversity in this church plant. We liked that the maskers and nonmaskers coexisted without making a political issue out of it. We weren't connecting though. It's hard to be vulnerable in these spaces. What we needed were personal invitations, not programs. We needed people who wanted to get to know us. We had the pastor and his wife over for dinner, and it went well. But we stalled out after that.

We were starving for some substance in the liturgy. There was only singing and a sermon. Not even a congregational prayer or benediction. We were also starving for substance in the sermon. The pattern seemed to be topical series of self-actualization with the help of a New Testament passage each week. It was better than the many other nondenoms that we visited with Christian nationalist tropes, but not much. The preaching wasn't really giving us Christ. I've learned that a lot of pastors of nondenoms who want to minister to those disillusioned are hitching onto popular philosophy that unhitches them from the Old Testament. We are missing the juice of the whole metanarrative of Scripture.

I love that juice. Like the disciples hearing about it from the resurrected Jesus on their seven mile walk to Emmaus, my heart burns for it.

That February my body broke out in hives. I think it was anxiety from this church homelessness. We had exhausted the nondenoms around us. (Some before even attending. I'm looking at you, church with a dispensational end-times view as part of the statement of faith on your website.) So many churches were eliminated for their denominational track record with abuse and cover-up (I'm looking at you,

Southern Baptist Convention) or patriarchal hierarchy (no more, no more). The worst part isn't my own longing and loneliness for church belonging. The worst part is that our youngest was turning eighteen, and I was experiencing this growing feeling that we failed to show him and our two daughters beauty in Christ's church. This is our last chance. Where is it? I pleaded with God about this.

We kept looking. In our search, we've seen numbness, starchiness, rigidity, spaces with the life sucked out of them, try-hards to make church cool, the gospel being made into a gimmick, weirdos, deceit, spiritual abuse, apathy, hate, the institution, corruption, and complete deconstruction.

I know church is for weirdos too, but why are there so many? As if Christianity turns you into one? Or worse. We've seen the worse.

February 11, 2023

This therapist guy that I've been binging podcast episodes on said that we just need to let it rip when we are angry with you, God. He spent a lot of time showing how Job did that. I mean, it's not like you don't know our complex emotions. We are the ones that won't face them. And you give us the words, even, in your Word. The whole time he was talking, I thought about C. S. Lewis's *Till We Have Faces*. And sure enough, he went there too at the end of the episode. To Orual before the gods. I've been thinking about that title a lot, and all that it means.

It feels so wrong to dig that anger out. But it won't stay in. If *The Body Keeps the Score*,¹ mine is starting to break out in hives. The internet says it's eczema. But the colloidal oatmeal isn't doing the trick. Then there's the eye twitch that's been questioning my sanity for the last week. Every spasm asks the question.

So I thought about whether I was angry at God while running my Monday grocery errands, because good, contemplative thinking sometimes happens in the car. I was afraid to be angry with God. How dare I, after all he gives? And all he is! Where is the gratitude? The Good Me is never angry at God. But she isn't real. God loves the real me. In this inner struggle, the fear in my cistern showed itself. The panic of feeling abandoned after the divorce rushed back. *Wait, do I fear God abandoning me? And not just the Presbyterian church? Am I afraid that me and my family will forever be on the outside of the body of Christ? Maybe we will even lose our longing.* There's been no sense of belonging in any of the churches we've tried. It's so easy for us now to see what's "wrong." Will we just become hardened?

My own hope mocks me now. She's so battered, who can blame her?

Maybe you're revealing to me how quickly I fall apart. How spoiled I am. How weak I am. Here I am, itching and twitching while my kids are about to fly right out of this nest forever. Thinking about how crazy their mom was for trying too hard to find a place for us in church. Knowing how hypocritical the people were. The preachers, the elders, the friends . . .

Maybe I'm mad because it feels like I've written these books and taught my kids and it's all coming up empty. I thought I was doing holy work. Would it have been better if I just served beer down the road? There's honor in that. The peopling.

I've been blacklisted from all the places I used to care about. Not that I want in anymore. What good did it do? They've reorganized their narrative and continue on without the troublemaker. The disrupter.

"Mom, can I say something? I think you are stressing yourself out over this church situation. I see how it is weighing on you. I see your anxiety over it. It's so heavy. We are going to be okay; you don't need to hold this all."

We were sitting at our local brewery having our Friday night burgers and beer. I was seen by my daughter. And she spoke into it. She was right. We are doing what we can. Do I really believe God will meet us here too? Do I believe that he can reach my kids, who've developed fantastic bullshit detectors when we walk through church doors? They've seen the "put-on-ness" in church after church that we've visited. I'm terrified that they've lost hope in what is real.

Will we find the resurrected Christ in any of the churches around us?

February 11, 2023

Today is Saturday. It seems Jesus is in the grave.

I know that isn't true. He's shown me himself and new life over and over. That's why I'm still listening and looking (Song 2:8). The words of a father begging Jesus for compassion for his son—if Jesus can do anything—rang in my mind: "I do believe; help my unbelief!" (Mark 9:24). Is there a more real prayer than that? Why does it take a boy possessed with demons for us to dig it out of us? Or years stumbling about in church searching for the resurrected Christ? Even as I encounter glimpses, and I know there are many in these churches looking for Christ, aching for Christ, and experiencing his presence.

I believe in Christ's church because she is covenantally united to him; she is his body. I believe in the total Christ, Christ and his church. That is why he created. That is why he became flesh. This reality of the total Christ, his unitive love, is why he went to the grave with our death. His church is his bride. She is a gift to him from the Father by the Spirit. She is risen with him and rising with him.

Lord, help my unbelief. Your church is fading from my vision. I need to just look to you. My prayers are being strangled by my unbelief. Each time I think you've set something up for me, a new hope, gathering my family on Sunday morning to look for you with me, we are deflated. And I do that stupid thing us Christians are trained to do—looking for the good in this, scrambling for purpose and meaningfulness in the disappointment, the lesson that we are supposed to learn, the blessings that we are supposed to be thankful for so that you will give us the blessing that we are asking for.

You are the blessing.

Today is Saturday. The doom of Saturday. I can't even find the garden where they have you. So I will just be sad. And mad. Put The Good Me in the grave with you. And pray for my unbelief—that my lament will not turn to despair.

Hold us here, Lord. Meet us here.

Seven

COMMUNING WITH ETERNITY

After nine months of wondering and dreaming; imagining the forming organs, skeleton, skin, fingerprints; feeling my belly as this alien inside me tumbled and hiccupped; shopping for the cutest darn outfits a little Byrdie can wear; flipping through name books, feeling the pressure of getting it just right; and painting her nursery full of Dr. Seuss characters, it was time. After calling my sister over to braid my hair, battling with a husband who wanted me out of his care and into the hospital's as soon as possible, questioning whether I can actually do this as the pain shockingly intensified, realizing there's no turning back, discovering the comfort of foot rubbing to help me cope, being angry and terrified that I needed better coping mechanisms than foot massage, cursing at my husband for answering the phone as if life was normal, and pushing, pushing, pushing a human being out of my own body, it was time. The time that is forever imprinted in my memory. The *here I am* moment when our faces met. She was looking for me, and when our faces met, we found each other. Solanna. Sunshine. Born on a Sunday.

When I became pregnant with our second daughter, I was full of joy. I couldn't wait to meet her. All the dreaming and planning was glorious. But I was also afraid. The love for our firstborn was so strong and so transformative. Could I love anyone else this much? Does she get the seconds? Zaidee broke my water to announce her impending arrival. That is so her. The panic hit me because now I knew what I was about to go through. It's time. We have to go through it. Nothing like starting a life with the trauma-bonding of childbirth. We go to war for each other. And then eternity broke in a second time. That *here I am* moment as she is out, placed on my chest, still warm from my insides. She was looking for me looking for her. I delighted in a whole new life. My heart filled full with more love than it could hold so that it had to be given away.

I had to seduce my husband for number three. Those girls had him tied around their fingers, and he didn't know if he could keep the gig up with a third. We already learned that love isn't like a pie that gets fractioned out. That's exactly what Matt was worried about. He knew his love would grow, but he wasn't so confident about the money and the sanity needed to navigate that. And there he was again, in just as much of a rush to get me out of the house and into the hospital when the labor began. Same battle. Same insane speeding down the highway. But he knew not to answer the phone during a contraction or to beg me to take the drugs this time. Haydn's *here I am* seemed more desperate than the others. Like his eyes were already telling me how sensitive his soul is to the indifference in the world. Like he was asking me if I see it—not just him, but the pain of life, the pain of missing the encounters, the pain of not being present to the *here I am*. I'm here, buddy; we'll do this together.

HERE I AM

The fracture, in our faces, in the world, is in not being able to see what's real and commune with it.[1] Then we ignore our imaginations as gifts that point us in the right direction. We live among common pieces—the handmade mug holding our craft roasted coffee, the indoor plants pointing to the rising sun, the mushrooms peeking out beside the driveway, even the dang bee we are swatting away while trying to get to the car—but we don't behold them. We don't hear them. We interact with grocery clerks, teachers, children, neighbors, UPS delivery drivers, baristas, the person waiting for you to finish on the StairMaster, and we don't see one another as eternal beings. We miss God shouting *here I am!* all day long. Barbara Brown Taylor tells us that "earth is so thick with divine possibility that it is a wonder we can walk anywhere without cracking our shins on altars."[2] And I believe it.

Sometimes I slip out to our front stoop to pray. The physical change of scenery symbolizes something in my spirit, a movement from inside my busy, distracting household to nature and fresh air. I can pause and just observe, feeling the morning sun on my skin. Maybe it will enlighten my soul as well. This time I was trying to slow my mind down. It was waking me up again at 2:00 a.m., firing random thoughts like fireworks, demanding my attention. That cycle is hard to break.

As I prayed about it, I noticed for the second day in a row

all the ants working so hard on the stoop, down the steps, on the walkway, and in the mulch. The day before, I was thinking how there was a metaphor there. And then it hit me. The ants were like my thoughts, working hard, going in all directions, ruminating over the stresses of the next day or week—work, travel, performance. They are all the things, the busy things, and the anxiety in them. But the ants can't see the big, beautiful tree in the yard, screaming *here I am!* in all its glory. They have such limited perception. Amazing little creatures they are, but their world is very small.

I know Proverbs encourages us to look to the ant for our work ethic (Prov. 6:6–8). But I felt God was directing my attention to these ants to help me chill out. They reminded me how small my world of anxieties really is and warned me not to miss the beauty God wants to show me. Right there, in that tree in my yard, with the sun on my skin, seeing the patterns of the ants' busyness, that became the prayer: grateful beholding, delighting, and letting God speak through it all. I needed to reorient myself because eternity was in the smells, sights, and feelings I was experiencing that very moment. My world expanding even as I saw how very small it was.

Church is not the only place to commune with God. Our worship services are a special communal summons, covenantally calling us out of our busyness to respond *here I am*. But there's also a divine liturgy happening throughout our day. This is what we are after in our spiritual formation: communing with what's real and eternal. Our faces are called to search for meaningfulness in the faces of others. To do this, we need to get behind the countenance, the mask, of one another's faces, finding that *here I am* present.

In the faces of others, God beckons us. If we will behold

the faces before us, maybe we can hear God saying, "Where are you?" We think we are too fractured to answer for ourselves, so we rarely listen. How terrifying would it be if we could hear the actual voice of God saying this? Who could bear it? But we see him prompt this liturgy over and over in his Word, starting with Adam and Eve. It doesn't take long in our poetic narrative to see that the first humans screwed up their commission, damning us all. Their eyes are opened, but not in the way they had hoped. They see they are naked, and that's now a problem. A vulnerable, terrifying problem. They do not want God to see them like this. But he's coming. They hide behind some trees. The comedy here in the midst of the suspense is really something. But what does God do? He asks, "Where are you?" (Gen. 3:9). That loaded question is meant to penetrate our souls. Can we answer that question? What kind of trees are we hiding behind to distract us from the eternal?

The divine call of God's "Where are you?" initiates a liturgical response. The original readers would recognize that the Hebrew *'ayyekkah?* ("Where are you?") is to be answered with *hineni* ("Here I am!"). It is a yes to God, an "I am ready" or "at your service." But that isn't how they answer. Where are Adam and Eve? They are far from God. A great chasm of transgression separates them. They are naked and exposed, blame shifting, without a proper covering. They are out of blessed communion with God and one another.

We see this *here I am* response in significant turning points in the Old Testament. *Here I am* is a response of faith. When God tests Abraham, he calls him by name, and Abraham's response in faith is, "Here I am" (Gen. 22:1). It's as if he is saying, "You are my God." And I don't understand one bit about what God tells him to do. I have all the theological answers about the testing of his faith, how it points to Christ, and the hints in the text that maybe Abraham's faith was strong enough to know God would provide another sacrifice (Gen. 22:5, 8). Either way, he doesn't tell his wife what he's up to. And I still wrestle with the fact that God tells him to bring his son Isaac as a burnt offering. But Abraham's faith and his *here I am* remain strong. Abraham brings Isaac all the way to the altar before he hears God call his name again. This time the angel of the Lord calls his name twice, "Abraham, Abraham!" And he answers, "Here I am." The Lord then provides a ram as the sacrifice in place of his son. Like Abraham, Jacob responds to God's summons twice with "Here I am" (Gen. 31:11; 46:2). In transformative moments of their lives, Moses, Samuel, and Isaiah also respond, "Here I am" to God's direct call (Ex. 3:4; 1 Sam. 3:1–10; Isa. 6:8). All of these men answer, "*Hineni.* I'm at your service."[3]

Can we answer this way? Do we even hear the call? Can we be present enough to make sense out of this echo resounding from the trees and the ants and in one another's faces? Isn't there a part of us longing for God to ask and a part terrified of what he will say if we answer? *Where are you?* Do we even want to see ourselves in the truth and condition of where we are? And do we really want to answer *here I am*? Jewish scholar Abraham Joshua Heschel poetically describes our lifelong fog in listening:

> In our own lives, the voice of God speaks slowly, a syllable at a time. Reaching the peak of years, dispelling some of our intimate illusions and learning how to spell the meaning of life-experiences backwards, some of us discover how the scattered syllables form a single phrase.

Those who know that this life of ours takes place in a world that is not all to be explained in human terms; that every moment is a carefully concealed act of His creation, cannot but ask: is there anything wherein His voice is not suppressed? Is there anything wherein His creation is not concealed?[4]

As Barbara Brown Taylor told us, divine possibility is everywhere. We should be cracking our shins like crazy! And yet it's so hard for us to see and hear and so hard for us to answer. God knows this more than we do. So he promises that we will know him: "Therefore my people will know my name; therefore they will know on that day that I am he who says, 'Here I am'" (Isa. 52:6). God says *hineni*! Can you believe it? We need him to. He says that he will answer us when we cry out; he will say, "Here I am" (Isa. 58:9). Even by those who did not ask or seek (Isa. 65:1). We see this promise fulfilled in Christ who hears us, stands before a holy God, and answers the call with his whole self, bringing us before the Father, "Here am I, and the children God has given me" (Heb. 2:13 NIV).

CRACKING SHINS IN THE HIGH SCHOOL PARKING LOT

April 28, 2023

If only I could make an altar with a stack of rocks in a Brunswick High School parking space, I would. To remind me and all the busy high schoolers, custodians, teachers, bus drivers, and administrators how God shows up in the ordinary, tedious moments of our day. How an unplanned annoyance revealed the playfulness and love that is in our cisterns. How withness is holiness. How I saw the absolute beauty of my family in the pouring down rain. The picture you gave me this morning, Lord. What a glory to behold.

It happened on a Friday morning. It was pouring down rain, and that was the forecast for the whole day. I rolled out of bed, got my coffee, and talked to my son, Haydn, a little before he left for school. It was senior prom day, and he was going to be driving his date all the way to Gaithersburg for dinner. Just what I needed—to worry about him driving a half hour out of town in a rainstorm at night. I chose not to show my anxiety and give him the freedom of being eighteen. I knew my girls would both point out how I would have never let them do that.

Five minutes after he left, he sent me a text saying that his tire-pressure sensor came on and the tire looked like it was going flat. Of all days. He took the bus from his home-base high school to the school that hosts his art program, and I woke up Matt to break the bad news. He developed a plan to go to the high school before work, put on the spare tire, and then try to leave work early to find the leak and fix the tire before prom. I decided to go as well to hold an umbrella for Matt. We drove two cars, as he was planning to go to work from there. We arrived at the high school parking lot only to realize we forgot Haydn's car keys. I immediately went back to get them and got stuck behind a neighborhood bus. Finally, I made it back with the keys, and Matt popped Haydn's trunk to get the spare tire. Rain was pounding on the umbrella. Our shoes were deep in puddles, the bottoms of our pants soaking. Haydn's trunk is full of junk—sneakers, deodorant, clothes, tennis racket—making it difficult to get to the spare. Matt shoved all the junk to the back to get the tire from the storage underneath, jacked the car up, and got to work. There was no way he was staying dry, but I did my best with the umbrella. He got the tire on, lowered the jack, and . . . the spare was going flat too. Of course.

Trying to get together a plan B in the pouring rain, Matt throws the original flat tire in the back of his truck and says he needs to go home and change now before work. Thankfully, he didn't have kids in his classroom during first period that day, and he called his teammates about the drama to say he may be a little late. We drove back. He pulled Haydn's tire out of his truck and found a screw lodged in it. He decided to go ahead and fix the tire now since he was already late and wet. The next thing you knew, our neighbor Steve was walking over in the rain with his air compressor. Matt plugged the tire, he and Steve filled it up, and we were headed back to the high school to put it on. It was still pouring. Back again with the jack, taking off the spare, me holding the umbrella. And Matt said, "Can you believe we are doing all this right now first thing in the morning? What a way to start the day!" I flirted a little, responding how it was kind of hot seeing him save Haydn's day like this, working on the car in the rain. I saw that humble half-smile of his as he let out a chuckle. He got the repaired tire on but still needed to go home and change. When we pulled our two cars into the driveway, he informed me that he just ate the wrap I packed for his lunch. Turns out all that tire changing made him hungry.

We ran up to the bedroom, giggling while taking all our wet clothes off. A couple of kisses and a new outfit later, I made my way back to the kitchen to make that man another wrap.

Just another day in paradise. Truly, I love it.

Looking back now, I see Haydn's text was a *Where are you?* call from God. And that parking space holding his flat tire was an altar where God was hiding in plain sight. At first, my answer was, "I am irritated and inconvenienced." I was about to have my house emptied so I could start my writing for the day. Thankfully, I was able to toss that irritation out of my cistern. Matt and I showed up—*here I am*—for Haydn. Matt didn't want to be late for work. We didn't want to get soaked. But as the situation got more and more inconvenient, the Spirit of God was beckoning some beautiful fruit out of our years of ordinary married love. The teamwork, the playfulness, getting drenched, fixing the flat, and Matt eating his lunch at 8:00 a.m. was all like a song singing, "This is who we are; this is who we are for each other. I see your face and you see mine. And I love where we are together."

Most of the time I feel like I'm having to do the work of facing the junk that is in my cistern. On that day, April 28, 2023, God called to us from the Brunswick High School parking lot, revealing the good work he was filling us with, revealing the holiness in the withness, and inviting us to commune with eternity before work.

Turns out, God really does care to take the time to find us each a parking space.

Eight

THE GAZE THAT DOES US IN

Why am I here? Do these people know what I did? Do they know about my so-called courage to follow Jesus and then my cowardice being revealed, just as he said it would be? Do they know about my absolute betrayal? *Is it me?* Am I the one he was talking about when we were drinking wine at our last meal together? Am I the fool for saying I would die with him? He knows who I really am. I'm the one hidden behind a mask of bravery, the one that looks away from him and sinks into the water. He prayed that my faith would not fail. But it did, just as he predicted. That very day, before the third crow of the rooster, I would deny even knowing him, not once, but three times. He knew.[1]

I saw his face looking at my face when I denied him. Looking at my self revealed. Just as he said. And yet the look in his eyes was love. Who could bear it? His love looking into me, knowing what I was hiding from myself. From him. From all of us who were at the table together.

I have to get out of here before I fall apart. I need to weep bitterly.

I can't bear myself. That the last thing Jesus saw of me was so true and awful and empty, so completely bankrupt. One of the last things he shared with us is how we stood by him in his trials,[2] and I didn't end up being one of the "we." He called us friends,[3] and I said I didn't know him. I didn't wake to pray with him as he was anguished in the garden.[4] How could I sleep through that? We were exhausted from *our* grief when he was agonizing before the Father. He needed us. I could have roused the rest. What if I would have prayed not to fall into temptation, like he said I would? Would it have changed what I did? Would I have stood by him? Would I be able to make better sense of what happened to him?

Where am I? What am I doing here gathered as one of the Eleven? We are disillusioned together, but do they think I even belong here to mourn with them? Am I any better than Judas? What's keeping me here with these people? Where else do I go? *To whom will we go?* That question echoes the very words I said face-to-face with Jesus when he looked at us and asked if we would desert him like the many others. I confessed to him that he was the Holy One of God.[5] Is he who I thought he was?

Who else could he be? The miracles I saw! My own mother-in-law was healed. He cast out demons. He gave us the authority to do the same.[6] I don't know what it means. When he first laid eyes on me, he named me "rock."[7] I wanted to believe that about myself—a nobody who was really a rock. Fear gripped me when he took my boat, teaching the crowds from it, and when we filled our nets overflowing with fish. Our nets were tearing with fish and our boats were sinking. I knew then that I wasn't worthy. And yet he renamed my vocation as a fisher of men! I left everything to follow him after that, to find out what that means. Now his gaze across the courtyard of the high priest's house when I denied him is burned into my memory, alongside my memory of the glow of his face shining like the sun, when Moses and Elijah appeared and a voice from heaven said, "This is my beloved Son, with whom I am well-pleased. Listen to him!"[8] The stupid things I said! It was too much to behold!

I hold all the looks that he gave me. The way his face drew out who I was. I can't get the love in his gaze out of my head. That final look should have shown me disgust and condemnation as I denied him, just as he said I would. He needed what I could not give before he faced complete darkness and death. Goodness incarnate was about to be desecrated and crucified between two criminals. He was paraded before those who mocked him. He had to bear the sight of his mother seeing it all. How can I be so consumed with the look he gave *me* knowing what face his mother, much braver than I, beheld?

Why did I run? Where do I go now? I'm covered in shame. Am I a total fraud? An imposter? Everything I thought I knew about the Messiah doesn't add up. I can't put words to my grief.

THE INTERRUPTION OF THE WOMEN

What is that noise? I can't handle these women right now; I cannot face them. Why are they so excited? I don't know that world anymore. The nonsense of their words is being muffled by the commotion. They are saying something about the grave being empty and not to look for the living among the dead—and that Jesus has risen! John and I take off. We must see what this is all about. But he gets ahead of me. Maybe there is a hesitation in my running. My heart is pounding, my throat is closing, and I don't know if I'm ready to see whatever this is. John is stopped short of the tomb, mouth agape. I cross the threshold into the tomb. I need to be in there, standing amazed among the folded cloths that Jesus died in. No Jesus in sight.[9]

We go back to tell the others. But why are we so afraid that we sit behind locked doors while Mary Magdalene remains where our Lord's body last was? As if the locked doors can stop what will happen next.

WHAT HAPPENS NEXT

His face. In our room. His whole body. Flesh and bones, speaking "Peace to you!" Just like that. Of all the possibilities of what would happen next, this one is beyond comprehension. Am I dead? About to die? He asks why we are troubled. Why do we doubt what is before our eyes? He asks for food to prove he is no ghost. And then he resurrects our understanding of God's plan. He helps us see how it's written in our Scriptures and how we are a part of it. He breathes on us the Holy Spirit and the power of forgiveness.[10]

THE POWER OF FORGIVENESS

Longing burns within me, but so does shame. The shame of the me that revealed himself just days ago. I can't reconcile it all. My boat helps me think. So I go fishing, doing what I know, what I was doing when Jesus called me. Why would he come to someone like me? Now I'm back to my old self, catching nothing all night long.

Until we hear someone say, "Friends, you don't have any fish, do you?"[11] In more ways than one, we don't. Something is the same and something is very different. The scene, no fish, listening to his absurd advice, the overwhelming number of fish that fill the nets. The net was not torn this time. It's a reminder of who he is, and of who I am in him, and a chance to rewrite the story I am telling myself. But John is the first to recognize him. As soon as he tells me it is the Lord, I can't wait to get to shore. I leap out of the boat into the sea.

We eat together. He looks at me again and sees the shame clinging to my absolute delight in his presence.

> Simon, son of John, do you love me?
> Simon, son of John, do you love me?
> Simon, son of John, do you love me?

And I realized, more deeply with each question, he does know. I had to see my fears for what they were: my delusions, the ways I wanted to manage him, my fractured self. But that's not who I really am. My soul had to die to those things. But first, it had to know they were there. He makes me with his gaze. It undoes and resurrects. He knows everything. And all I need to know is this one thing. That's why I'm here. That's where I am.

> Yes, Lord, you know that I love you.
> Yes, Lord, you know that I love you.
> Yes, Lord, you know that I love you.[12]

Part Three

THE BLESSED
FACE

Nine

GOD SHOWED US HIS FACE

May the LORD bless you and protect you;
may the LORD make his face shine on you and
be gracious to you;
may the LORD look with favor on you and give
you peace.
—Numbers 6:24-27

I can't tell you how many times I've heard this benediction
at the end of a worship service. It goes so far back in my
memories, recalling when I first learned it would be like
recalling when I first learned the alphabet or the "Now I lay
me down to sleep" bedtime prayer (that for the longest time,
I thought began, "Now I'm Aimee down to sleep . . ."). This
blessing is like turning the pages of the days of my life. I grew
up Southern Baptist, and this benediction could be counted
on to close us out of the service as much as the doxology we
sang after we gave our offerings. It was the background noise

that I didn't pay attention to at first; it meant the service was ending. But I did pick up on the sacredness of it. We were being blessed before we left. I held still like I did when my grandma was pinning one of her broaches on me or when my mom was braiding my hair. You need to stay in the flow. Moving may cause unintended pain. Let the masters do their work. And walk away beautified.

Later, I began to think about the words. God's face shining upon me—this was the blessing. And yet it was so elusive. So was the man saying it. The closest I ever got to my pastor besides that awkward handshake or smile on our way through the exit door was when I was baptized at eight years old. I was nervous about screwing it up somehow and of the holiness of it all. Until I saw my pastor, the man I only ever saw in a suit, with his comb-over perfectly hair-sprayed into place. He was standing in our church bathtub, where many others before me gave themselves to the Lord in baptism, wearing knee-high rubber boots over his pants. I never knew about the boots. You don't see those from the pews. It's insider knowledge. I gained more insider knowledge: there's a bar in the tub that you lock your feet under so they don't decide to whirl themselves into the air as you're dunked. While everyone else watches you clothed in your white robe die to your old life and rise to a new life in Christ, they don't see you afterward in the bathroom blow-drying your hair, chitchatting with the other newly baptized, reprimping to return not-so-nonchalantly to the worship service with your new glow, ready to be the one shaking hands after the service. My friend Jess and I saw things differently after we were baptized. We giggled about the rubber boots, whispering all of our behind-the-curtain revelations to one another. Those rubber boots humanized our pastor. But they also kept him a little too dry, still separated from our full immersion. After all, he didn't have the time for postbaptismal primping during worship. Now we were insiders.

That's when I began thinking about the face of God shining upon me. Where was it? I knew it was important. I needed it. I'd gone through the community's rites of passage to receive it. But no one ever talked about it. What was this big deal that was never discussed? To be honest, there could have been whole sermons about it, but I was too busy imagining what my pastor would look like if he combed his hair the other way, or what it would be like to swing from the chandeliers off the balcony, to pay proper attention. I can tell you that now, many years later, visiting numerous churches in search of a place to belong, it's shocking to find the lack of benediction given. And it's sad. I need—long for—this blessing.

GENERATIONS OF BLESSINGS

Now I'm Aimee down to sleep,
I pray the Lord my soul to keep,
And if I die before I wake,
I pray the Lord my soul to take.
God bless: Mom, Dad, Luke, Brooke, Grandma,
Pap Pap, Grandma, Grandad . . .

. . . and the ridiculously long list of extended family and friends continued. You don't want to leave anyone out of God's blessings. My sister developed an amazing skill to rattle off her list of names for God to bless at lightning speed, like it was all one word. When she finished, we'd burst out laughing at her mad skills.

This prayer comforted us and terrified us, which is why most of Gen Xers and millennials did not pass it down to their children. Why in the world would any parent who wants their child to actually go to sleep when they put them to bed teach them to throw, "If I die before I wake," into their nighttime prayer routine? Bad idea! The anxiety that thought produced wasn't helping anyone go to sleep. The following generations had the gumption to not follow our Puritan forefathers, who were obsessed with morbidity, in freaking out our children right before they are supposed to surrender to the death of their day. I can see why the prayer took for so many generations, though. The second part, "I pray the Lord my soul to take," became a sort of superstition. What happens if you *don't* say it?

But we were happy to move onto the blessings. And that is what a benediction is: a supernatural blessing from God that sends us off. He started the world that way. After he created man and woman, "God blessed them, and God said to them, 'Be fruitful, multiply, fill the earth, and subdue it. Rule the fish of the sea, the birds of the sky, and every creature that crawls on the earth'" (Gen. 1:28). The world began with God's blessing and sending out man and woman to his creation, bearing his image, to be blessings. To bless something is to pronounce it good. And we see that repeatedly in the creation account. God saw that the light was good; the land and the seas were good; the vegetation, plants, and trees were good; the sun, moon, and stars were good; the sea creatures and the birds were good; the wildlife, livestock, and creatures that crawl on the ground were good; man and woman created in the image of God were declared very good.[1] Bless, bless, bless!

Amazingly, we get to bless God as well. We see it all over Scripture. It is a Jewish tradition to pray *brakoth* throughout the day, prayers of blessing to God. The Song of Zechariah (found in Luke 1:68–72) is often referred to as the "Benedictus." It begins, "Blessed is the Lord, the God of Israel, because he has visited and provided redemption for his people" (v. 68). In Ephesians 3:20–21, we see, "Now to him who is able to do above and beyond all that we ask or think according to the power that works in us—to him be glory in the church and in Christ Jesus to all generations, forever and ever. Amen." Blessing God is a recognition of blessedness. When we are blessed, we are given his blessedness.

Don't we just long for blessing? From parents, friends, and especially God. I have deeply missed the blessing, the benediction, in worship at the churches we've been visiting. I miss being sent off with God's blessing.

You see benedictions all over the Epistles. They can be declarations or prayers. Benedictions can be simple, such as 2 Corinthians: "The grace of the Lord Jesus Christ, and the love of God, and the fellowship of the Holy Spirit be with you all" (13:13). And they can be elaborate, like in Hebrews: "Now may the God of peace, who brought up from the dead our Lord Jesus—the great Shepherd of the sheep—through the blood of the everlasting covenant, equip you with everything good to do his will, working in us what is pleasing in his sight, through Jesus Christ, to whom be glory forever and ever. Amen" (13:20–21). What a great conclusion to corporate worship—to be sent out with God's blessing on us and to be reminded of who we are in Christ and who we are to be to others. The Bible begins with blessing in the creation of the earth and humankind, and it ends with blessing in a vision of resurrection on the new heavens and the new earth: "The grace of the Lord Jesus be with everyone. Amen" (Rev. 22:21).

SHINY HAPPY FACES NEED NOT APPLY

Many pastors use the blessing that God instructed for Aaron and his sons to bless the Israelites, "May the LORD bless you and protect you; may the LORD make his face shine on you and be gracious to you; may the LORD look with favor on you and give you peace" (Num. 6:24–26), for the benediction at the end of worship. Isn't our deepest longing for God's face to shine upon us? Don't we want to receive his smile as he gazes at us? God's face shining upon us is transformative. I see the benediction of Numbers 6:26 as the ultimate blessing. In one sense we wait longingly for the day we see the face of God delighting in our face. But in that longing for the not-yet, we also have the already. Jesus is the face of God. The first thing the resurrected Jesus says when he appears to his disciples is "Peace be with you" (John 20:19, 21, 26). Peace is literally with them. The blessing has visited them in the resurrected flesh. He has done it. And he gives himself.

How do we think about the face of Jesus? With his glory masked in flesh, we learn that "he didn't have an impressive form or majesty that we should look at him, no appearance that we should desire him" (Isa. 53:2). Except for the transfiguration, where he revealed his glory before Peter, James, and John,[2] and John's postascension vision in Revelation,[3] Jesus's radiance was veiled.

If we want to see the face of God, we are to look to the incarnate and resurrected face of Jesus the Christ. And we are to be the face of Christ for one another. We can only behold the face of Jesus spiritually on this side of the resurrection. But God did show us his face in Christ, and we are to seek it still today. Our beings cry out for it. So what does that look like? How does the church look after we're given the blessing of the Lord's face shining upon us?

We learn that "the Son is the radiance of God's glory and the exact expression of his nature,"[4] and we believe that our faces need to testify to this as his people, his bride. But how do we reconcile the radiance and the ordinary in the face of Jesus and how that juxtaposition affects our own faces now? It is easy to try to "put on" the face we think the church is supposed to have. After all, we want to bear the testimony of his goodness, and we want to look like the gospel is as transformative and life-giving as we believe it is. And yet we aren't as transformed as we would like to be. Not now, anyway. Too often, we do not feel like God's face is shining upon us. In fact, sometimes it feels like God is hiding his face.

So we put on our church faces. The Shiny Happy People[5] face that we put on when we get out of our cars and are greeted by another Shiny Happy Person. We push down our suffering, our dissatisfaction, the way we just snapped at our spouse, disappointment in our spiritual growth, and our pain, and we pretend as if we are put together. But what if the blessing is in the mess, and we are missing it while plastering a church face over it? How many Shiny Happy People do we see in Scripture? That's not what blessing looks like. It wasn't what Jesus looked like. So why is the church so full of them? If Jesus doesn't make Shiny Happy People, are we really sent out of the service with God's face shining upon us? What does that look like then? How do we get to God's face?

The answer is so thoroughly Christian. When we experience God's face shining upon us, we encounter resurrection. Yes, there is the future resurrection, that Great Day when we behold and are re-created in glorious consummation.

But it is breaking in now, and we can behold unceasing resurrections in our day—but only if we are willing to look at the darkness and hang out in the underground with the suffering, the disappointment, the shame, and all the other pains that we want to be distracted from or cover up. Christ's face doesn't skip over the deaths. So we can look into that darkness with one another and name it, grieve it, die to any expectations we wrongly placed on God or ourselves, and feel our need for Christ's intimate presence. And we will find Christ's face shining upon us. As Caryll Houselander explains, "Christ seems to have fallen in love with our suffering, so passionately has he laid hold of it and made it his." He entered into it all. "Christ has lived each of our lives, he has faced all our fears, suffered all our griefs, overcome all our temptations, labored in all our labors, loved in all our loves, died all our deaths." This is a blessing indeed! He is there! Because of this, "Our Christ-life is the life of the risen Christ."[6] Because Jesus has entered into our limitations, our poverty, our unrequited loves, sickness, and tragedies, the power of his resurrection is Eastering all over the place now.

> We are the resurrection, going on always, always giving back Christ's life to the world.
>
> In our sin, we are the tombs in which Christ lies dead, but at the first movement of sorrow for sin he rises from the dead in us, the life of the world is renewed by our sorrow, the soul that was in darkness radiates the morning light. In the moment that we are forgiven, the world is flooded with forgiveness.[7]

His face shining upon us radiates over all his creation. Bask in the love and power of this benediction when we rise, receiving this blessing, and go out into the world. This is why I haven't given up on looking for a church. I need to be able to walk into worship with a body of believers as my whole self. I need witness to all the ways I've struggled and failed in trying to be fully and gloriously human, one imprinted with the image of God, and to all the ways I've been harmed and harm others. We walk in with our real faces, our whole stories that need seen and held, sorting out what needs buried in the earth to await resurrection. We grieve the darkness, lament injustice, mourn our sin, and wait and watch together for Christ's face to shine upon us.

> Those who look to him are radiant with joy;
> their faces will never be ashamed. (Ps. 34:5)

WHAT A WOMAN PASTOR SHOWED ME

"Why don't you give one of the mainline churches a try? You might not line up with all of their doctrine and methods, but many are still faithfully preaching Christ, and you will at least be able to have a substantial liturgy."

A pastor-friend visiting from out of town said something like this to me and my husband while chatting with us on my patio. I let the idea linger for a while. What have we got to lose? I realized that one thing holding me back is what other people would think. I was worried about the "I told you Aimee was on a slippery slope" people and the "it's really sad that Aimee's trauma led her to unsound teaching" people. In other words, the people who were already talking badly about me or trying to pull me back into their own harmful systems.

So we visited the Methodist church in town. I never thought I would go to a Methodist church. The theological elitism remaining in me from my previous denomination didn't take them seriously. I heard they abandoned the gospel. On the way, I shot up one of those arrow prayers: "Lord, I am looking for Christ in your church. Help me see him if he's there."

He was.

It was an old church, a small congregation—which was mostly old as well, and all white. I appreciated the amount of mature people and was encouraged by some younger families. But we were hoping for a more ethnically diverse group to learn with and from. They were friendly. The older woman in sparkly sneakers was particularly interesting to me. I want some bling in my silver years. The music wasn't obnoxious but could use a little more umph. There was a mixture of hymns and contemporary music. No one was cool. Hallelujah! They followed the church calendar, and we were in the Lenten season. The liturgy was refreshing. Christ was there. The whole service was saturated in the gospel.

The pastor is a woman. She was out on maternity leave through the rest of the month. We decided to stick around, play it week by week, and experience it with the pastor there. She returned at the end of March.

March 26, 2023

I don't even know how to put into words the beauty, power, and simplicity of what we beheld as a family. We went back to that Methodist church, looking forward to a service with the pastor's return from her maternity leave. It all would sound so absurd to me only six months ago. Me, a Calvinist, walking into a Methodist church. A mainline church!

Me, looking forward to a woman pastor returning from maternity leave. God, you know all it took to put me here. The humiliation. The desperation. The schlepping our family from church to church looking for you. And here we are in this white, aging congregation. Who just a few years ago brought in this young woman pastor, educated at Princeton Seminary, still growing her new family.

We walk in inhaling the smell of bacon and maple syrup as the congregation is hosting a breakfast immediately following the service to welcome Pastor Katie and her family back. We aren't going. It's too much for our first social event there. Although a few of the older women have invited us, I don't want to Aimee-pounce on this pastor at a breakfast where her congregants who missed her would like to be normal people. I'm still figuring out how to be a normal person.

I catch a glimpse of her talking to someone in the front row, with her three-month-old infant strapped to her chest. I wonder when she is going to unwrap him so that she can "go to work." She has soft-looking skin, naturally flowing light brown hair, no noticeable makeup, no vestments, wearing modest clothes, her collar covered by a baby harness. Little Wilbur is sleeping away on her chest. I hear her say something to her conversation partner about how this is his usual naptime and she hopes he will continue to sleep.

I notice that her husband is in the other pew in the front row. Their toddler is playing on the floor. This little boy, Howard, proved to be the child who likes to distract and be heard. He's wearing Vans sneakers. Oh man, that made me like them a little more.

The service starts. Katie calls us to worship, baby still strapped to her chest. Her voice is not put on. There's a smile on her face, and you can tell she is a little nervous.

Maybe even a little rusty after three months, in which time she pushed a baby out of her body and has been feeding him with it on demand. I've always liked the name Katie. During the prayer-request time before the congregational prayer, Katie tells us how good it is to be back and how much she missed everyone. One of the praises from an older woman in the back is about Katie's return but also about how smoothly everything ran in her absence. This is a mature congregation, and they don't depend on a one-woman show. It takes a mature leader to leave for three months knowing this, preparing them for this.

She moves onto the children's talk after the singing. I'm thinking surely the baby will be separated from his mother afterward. She sits with the children, talking with them about how Jesus wept. Wilber started to weep. Katie casually half-stands up and does the mommy-bounce that soothes little Wilber, not missing a beat in talking with the children and answering their questions. She then dismisses the little ones, who go to the children's time outside of the sanctuary, and transitions behind the pulpit *with baby Wilbur still on her chest.*

I watched a woman deliver a wonderful sermon with a baby attached to her.

I was attuned to the sermon on John 11—how Jesus is the resurrection and what that means for us in our own dark moments today. And Wilbur slept on her chest. It was a sight to behold. Just writing about it makes me think of the women in the fields working all day with a baby attached to them. But here is choice. Here is freedom. And this is what it looks like. I think about the men who have everything taken care of for them as they do "the most important service" of delivering the word of God to his people. And Katie showing something very different. Her voice was soft but engaging. Her speech was simple but intelligent. She not only knew what she was talking about but was talking to actual people.

We sang a couple more songs, and then it was time for the benediction. The children got out of their special time early and were finding their parents as Katie walked up to give the blessing. That's when Howard, her outspoken toddler, bypassed daddy and ran straight to his pastor-mom. As she was raising her arms, he began yelling, "No, Mommy; no, Mommy; no, Mommy!" over and over through the entire benediction. How hilarious! Don't bless these people, Mommy! She made a joke about how he needs to get acclimated again to the Sunday service. Me too, little buddy. Me too.

Ten

PROVOCATIONS TO BLESSING

Anticipation. He's about to arrive. When we've spent a week apart, when we were dating long distance, or at the end of our work day early in our marriage, I would get excited to see him, and I would think about Matt being excited to see me. Except that's not the greeting I usually received. There was me, filled with welcome, inhaling and holding my breath in for a pause, eyes growing and rising, the corners of my mouth rising, my whole body rising, looking for his face as he walked in the door. And then his face would barely raise, unable to meet the altitude of mine. This ambivalent face that hosted an inner war of wanting to free itself to delight but giving into hardening, distancing, and self-protecting. His face did not want to be disrupted by mine. I could see it. And it completely deflated me.

For years.

I longed for Matt's face to light up and match mine when he greeted me. I wanted him to smile at me with his cheeks and eyes and shoulders, to not be able to wait another second to kiss me, to embrace me as a gift. But I couldn't find him. I had to work to reach him. A monster of anxiety hides in my husband's soul, trying to suck the life out of him. For the longest time he was ashamed of it, unsuccessfully trying to mask it with that ambivalent face. He would act as if it's normal to come in the house aloof. Maybe it is. I'd give him space, act casual, and slowly draw him out of himself. Eventually, the greeting would come out of him too—completely unorthodox but much more to be savored. Beyond the welcome that I wished for, his greeting also said, "I can see you now, and you've helped me to see me." A moment of peace be with you.

I'm an affectionate person. I often fear I'm too much. So even though my husband has shown his affection and expressed his love for me on countless occasions, these reunions fed my fear that I really am too much, that I want too much. *He must be thinking about that before he opens the door.* It took a long time for me to be able to articulate my own disappointment and fear in this dynamic. And when I did, it grieved the man who loves me to learn how his entrance affected me. We've both done work here, and he's my favorite person to practice with.

MATT'S UNORTHODOX BENEDICTIONS

Our story started with this same dynamic. My aunt called me one day while I was at college, saying she found my husband. I know, the audacity of that statement. What was really going on was that my mom and all her sisters married right out of (or before in my mom's case) high school. That was their only way out. Her family had no plan for her or her sisters to go to college or advance in any other vocation that afforded them independence. I was the first on that side of the family to attend a university. So it was a real mystery in the eyes of my aunts (not my mom) that I was about to turn twenty—twenty!—and was not looking for a husband. I tried to explain my lack of interest in rushing into marriage. Sandra just kept telling me about him. He was her son's second grade teacher, and she was the parent volunteer. Then she mentions that she invited him to hear them sing at the nursing home the weekend I was coming home for a visit. The *them* is my aunts and my mom. The four sisters harmonize beautifully together, and they would sing gospel music in churches, nursing homes, and wherever people could be blessed by it.

So now I was stuck with this embarrassing encounter. This Matt guy is probably thinking I'm some desperate niece. To this day, I cannot believe he accepted the invitation. I think he was just being nice and trying to get his parent volunteer off his back, but he also may have been curious if maybe 80 percent of the praises she was harping on about me were true. He walked into the nursing home and barely looked at me when Sandra introduced us. Okay, good, this won't be too much of a thing. I won't have to deal with some eager try-hard. We both awkwardly sat there watching them warm up. The sisters often sang acapella, but this older guy who sometimes played acoustic guitar for them was there. He creeped me out a bit. Which is why, when the first real words mumbled out of Matt's mouth were, "Who invited Dennis Hopper?" I about died laughing. The 1994 movie *Speed* had released the year before, where Dennis Hopper played the creepy, extortionist bomber. This guitar player looked just like him. But it was more than that. Matt's comment and delivery revealed that he saw the same creepiness as me, and he probably picked up on me seeing it before he cracked the joke. Even though he barely looked at me when we were introduced, I was seen. A beautifully unorthodox benediction. Bless this connection that we both see what's off here. Let's welcome the humor of it all together.

It happened again the second time we were in the same room. My aunts get even weirder, so consider yourself warned. About six weeks passed, and I was coming home for Christmas break. Aunt Becky was having a Christmas party. She tells me that she's found the perfect guy for me. Seriously. And she invited him to the party. "You'll love him, Aimee. He wears a cowboy hat." This was during one of my eclectic stages where I was blending my hippie style with some cowgirl. (I say this as if I grew out of it.) His name was Jay.

JAY. "People call me Jaybird."

Strike one.

But guess what? Sandra also invited Matt to the Christmas party. I hadn't talked to him since we all went back to my mom's house for a meal after the nursing home that day. Matt and I had shared a ride on mom's four-wheeler across her seven acres of land and had good conversation getting to know each other. Sandra kept telling me to call him after that, saying he was talking about me. But I didn't want to be aggressive about it. I had a good time, enjoyed his company, was a bit curious to know him more, but the ball was in his court. Now the plot thickened. Matt arrived, and if he said hello, I don't remember it. Certainly his face didn't light up with a, "Glad to see you!" But he came.

Long story short, Jaybird followed me around like he had taken some Dale Carnegie "How to Make Friends" course, asking ridiculous questions.

JAYBIRD. "If you could travel anywhere in the world right now, where would you go?"

ME. "Australia."

JAYBIRD. "That's funny, the guy over there said the same thing," pointing to Matt.

At the time, I had a year and a half left of college and was realizing that I didn't really want to be a teacher anymore. This wasn't acceptable to Jaybird. He wanted to fix my life for me.

JAYBIRD, *following me around as I'm trying to politely walk away.* "You know what you need? You need a nice blanket and a picnic basket with me where we can sit by a pond and figure out what you are going to do with the rest of your life."

ME, *not even trying to disguise the "Who in the hell does this guy think he is?" look on my face.*

MATT, *in ear shot of this scene.* "She's going to open up a coffee café."

A beautifully unorthodox benediction. I didn't remember that I told him that dream of mine on our four-wheeler ride. Bless this connection where we both are trying to swat away an idiot with the revelation of being truly heard and believed in. The real me was seen and welcomed. Bless this declaration of your support. The rest was history.[1]

WELCOMING A FACE

"Every encounter begins with a benediction."[1] While benediction, corporately understood, is the blessing and sending out at the end of the worship service, French philosopher Emmanuel Levinas speaks of welcoming a face with a benediction. He says this benediction is "contained in the word *bonjour*"[2] and explains all that this greeting represents. When we encounter another person, their otherness is a provocation to awaken our own face, our own otherness, in welcome. *Bonjour* is a blessing. It's a "Here I am," an "I am glad to see you." It prioritizes the other person.[3] But first you have to really see them. Not the rehearsed greeting we all do throughout the day without really attuning to the person. And there is so much power in this awakening, seeing, and blessing.

We receive that benediction as we are sent out of worship, but it is the first thing we anticipate on that Great Day when we behold God. The new age will begin with benediction. Think about the transformative power of the benediction from God's face. And how we image that now. Our faces provoke one another to welcome and bless. Levinas calls it an "ontological courtesy, being-for-the-other."[4] When I welcome you, I not only pronounce it good that you exist and are here, but I am joining in God's and all of creation's awareness of your goodness. We are imaging God when we,

---

1. And I did open that coffee shop a year after we married. Those were some really good times.

as we encounter one another, give recognition, welcome, and blessing. And we awaken one another in this way, calling forth our goodness. It is good that you are other. Your strangeness is only due to my own. You are not just like me, and our benedictions appeal to one another's uniqueness and to one another's vocation to love. This provocation to love, and to recognize the dignity of the other, summons your own humanness. Your welcome and blessing of another recognizes that you are uniquely the one at that moment to answer to them.[5] You are *for* them. And in this way, "theology begins in the face of the neighbor." The face-to-face moment of an encounter is so much more than looking and greeting. The blessing is to see the act of God in the awakening to love. "God descends in the 'face' of the other."[6]

Jesus teaches us this in the Gospels. He tells us that whatever we do for the least of his brothers and sisters—the hungry, the thirsty, the stranger, the naked, the sick, the prisoner—we do to him. We are visiting Jesus. We are smiling at Jesus. We are welcoming Jesus. *Or* we are depriving Jesus. We are shunning Jesus. We are neglecting Jesus (Matt. 25:31–46). Our faces, as well as the faces of outcasts, are provocations to see the Lord and his goodness.

Lest we think that we are only to offer benediction to those we feel are worthy, Jesus tells us to "bless those who curse you" (Luke 6:28). This reveals something much deeper about blessing. It isn't about us. It's about the goodness that God gives. If we are to be conduits of his blessings, we need to realize that we are not managers of God. I struggle with how this blessing looks. I have been a people pleaser for most of my life, so it was a shock to my system to be cursed by so many spiritual leaders. Even their benedictions were curses to me. When I got an email from an authority in the church that began "Greetings in the name of our Lord and Savior, Jesus Christ," I knew how manipulative it was. We can be manipulative with our own benedictions. I don't want to do that.

How do I bless my enemies in a way that is genuine? We aren't really on speaking terms, and that boundary is healthy. They've proven themselves unsafe. Jesus isn't telling victims to welcome abuse. That doesn't bless either party. Remember, the blessing is seeing Christ in the other and the awakening of our true selves to love. All the unique colors of who we are come out in that.

Kate Bowler and Jessica Richie speak of how blessing is a language that resides with our agonies. "There is a beautiful and instructive language that we can use for naming that strange mix of awful and divine experiences in our lives."[7] Blessing is to be distinguished from praise: "The act of blessing is the strange and vital work of noticing what is true about God and ourselves. And sometimes those truths are awful. Like *blessed are those who mourn*."[8] What Jesus pronounces as blessings in his Sermon on the Mount doesn't feel true. "But in the act of blessing the world as it is and as it should be, we are starting to reassemble what we know. Maybe, God, you are here in the midst of this grief. Maybe, God, you can provide for this specific problem or be discoverable when I'm buttering this toast."[9] We aren't just slapping good words like masks over the terrible or the mundane. We are acknowledging what is true about God and ourselves in the grief. Tying that back into Levinas and seeing the face as a provocation to benediction, the blessing also acknowledges our vocation to love. Somehow. We can only do this if we join with God by his Spirit.

There's a lot of preparation I need to do in my own heart

for this. How would my face meet the face of my enemy if there was a chance encounter? What would this encounter draw out of me? What would I feel in looking at their face? How is God coming to me in these feelings? What does God want me to learn about myself and the other before me? There's a lot of prayerful work to do here. But it must be honest.

> Blessed is this struggle that leads me to look at my
>   sadness, my fears,
> that makes me ask what I really want.
> What my values are.
> To remember what I am becoming.
> Blessed is the agony of considering how to be for the
>   goodness of someone who's harmed me.
> Blessed is my own churning and turning to find you
>   in it, God.
> Blessed is your kindness that leads to repentance.
> You made this person; and you are good.
> You are kind to this person.
> Maybe I can just recognize that in their face.
> I give that to my enemies.
> Maybe the benediction is in letting them see my
>   vulnerable face looking at theirs.

We don't need a forced *bonjour*. But I'm not done. That's the great part about doing this work to prepare for an encounter. What comes out in the expressions on our faces reveals what is in our cisterns. What does my enemy draw out of my face, and what do I draw out of theirs? Does it line up with our values and what we love? We must regard one another in this encounter. Maybe I need to think more deeply about the humanness of my enemy. Irenaeus of Lyons famously wrote some two thousand years ago, "The glory of God is a human being fully alive." Maybe I need to search for what is alive in their face and alive in my own face.

> Blessed are you, God, for your goodness in bringing
> us to see what's real.
> Blessed are those who see.

I'm still working through this. But the gift of repentance, seeing what's real and turning toward that divine beauty of Christ's love for us, is such a powerful act of his grace and goodness toward us. Wanting our enemies to be fully alive is a start. Can I hold out hope for them along with hope for myself? Can I be brave enough to want us all to see the incongruencies between our knowledge of how glorious we and the whole world are to be and how we are turned the wrong way? These are the things we want, right? Don't we want to grow in the greatest commandment and the one that is just like it?

> "Teacher, which command in the law is the greatest?"
> He said to him, "Love the Lord your God with all your heart, with all your soul, and with all your mind. This is the greatest and most important command. The second is like it: Love your neighbor as yourself." (Matt. 22:36–39)

Why is the second greatest command like the first? Our love for one another is tied to our love for Christ. We find his love there in our neighbor. When we see their goodness, we find him. When we see their poverty, we find him. And we are found by him.

We miss getting to know Jesus in the people beside us or those worshiping with us. We miss getting to know ourselves as one loved by him too. And we miss what we are becoming. How do we think about heaven? Do we at all? Do we delight to think of unhindered, embodied communion with the triune God and one another? Do we have the freedom to see one another as we are loved by God and the freedom to love without fear, shame, jealousy, or any idea of scarcity? Are we free to create and learn and delight in the new earth, to see and know in our bones that we are delighted in by God and one another, and to forever express wonder in the grace of it all?

Maybe these encounters with one another invite us to see eternity breaking in now. To learn to think and love *with* God instead of just in what we know *about* him. Then we are joining with the Holy Spirit within us and one another. As Dallas Willard describes, "Heaven as it really is doesn't make a lot of sense to people, and it won't make a lot of sense except when understood in continuity with life experienced now, because in fact heaven is a continuation of life now. See, eternal life is not something that you get after you are dead. Eternal life is a way of living—now, even as we are alive."[10]

FUNCTIONAL ASSETS

Anticipation is usually exciting for me. Anticipation is anxiety producing for Matt. This difference had a lot to do with our aforementioned face-to-face encounters after being apart. It made me think further about the nature of anticipation. Matt grew up not knowing what to expect, imagining the worst scenarios and preparing himself for disappointment and loss. So he worked hard to keep others from seeing his vulnerabilities, like hope, delight, and longing. The very things I wanted to taste in his welcome kisses.

But with the trauma I went through in the church and in my vocation as a writer and speaker, I began to better understand where Matt was coming from. We open ourselves up to vulnerabilities during genuine encounters. And there is a lot to work through in wanting to bless and be a blessing without becoming performative or viewing it as a transactional relationship with God or one another.

I wanted to be a blessing in my church. A functional asset. Not one of those pew-warmers who slipped in and out as if they are there to be served. I wanted to serve in every way, to discover my gifts, to use them for God and for the gospel.

And we did, my husband and I. We probably started off stacking chairs after the service. There's nothing like stacking chairs in a church plant without its own building to make you feel like a helpful part of community. Then we started showing up to the picnic with the cookies and deviled eggs, volunteering for nursery duty, and giving the announcements. I didn't want to give the announcements. Not my comfort zone. I tried to explain this to our pastor.

I gave the announcements.

Then I started leading a women's Bible study, and Matt and I became the youth leaders for a while. Matt was the one you could depend on to help the seniors in the church with lawn needs—or really anything, especially keeping them company. He loved to bring some of the youth along to close the age gap and build relationships. Over the years, we hosted small groups, progressive dinners, and many parties. I served on committees, taught Sunday schools, greeted the lovely faces coming in the building, and attended Wednesday pizza nights and Bible studies. We often ended up closing the place down on Sunday afternoons, happy to see our friends and talking, talking, talking, until it was time for the lights to shut off. Matt was often the one asked to shut the lights off. Clever move.

That was us. Functional assets. We were *bizzy*. When we moved and changed churches, we'd jump right in.

Now we are awkward Sunday-morning seat warmers.

We are different people—more and less than our previous selves.

How do I put it into words? What does collective spiritual abuse do to a body and soul? Or to a family? What do you do when church no longer feels safe? We don't have the trust or the energy to be functional assets. We've lost interest in all the programs. The hustle of it all. How do I walk into a potluck dinner now, knowing I'm not known by these new people and maybe I never was by the old ones? The vulnerability makes my bones ache, and the longing to truly connect makes them cry out inside of me. I don't have the stamina to present any kind of church face. I can't even try to explain how I got there. As a pew warmer.

We get invited to the Sunday breakfasts, the outreach events—all the things. But not to coffee, lunch, or out for a beer. Not into personal lives. No real encounters. Is it because we are not functional assets? Do we even have the drive anymore to take the initiative?

Does anyone see Christ in us? Do they see me squirming to share during the corporate prayer requests but still feeling like an outsider? I'm not sure whether to let them in. Is that what keeps them at arm's length?

June 2, 2023

Finally we are in a church with more liturgy and less hierarchy. With warm faces. But they are collectively warm. The greetings are surface because they do not know us. And the benediction has a bitter after-taste when you know that awkward moment that will follow. There's a part of me that just wants to write a letter to the church. Maybe let them know how we are damaged goods—perhaps that will explain our keeping an arm's length. But from that, to let them know the courage it takes to keep trying. And how lonely it is to be standing there after the benediction in a church where we have no community. No one who knows us. No one trying—no personal invitations to meet up. Just to the church breakfast. Maybe I don't have the courage for the church breakfast yet. Who do we sit with? What do we reveal about ourselves? Will anyone ask?

Do you want to know what my functional asset is right now? Pew sitting. Uncomfortable pew sitting. Yet, in doing so, we are dying to a transactional way of thinking about spiritual maturity. Pew sitting challenges the ideas we had about our value. There is a pain and loneliness in not being known and in not serving—and the good Lord knows the many theological imaginations that are percolating in my mind, wanting to speak themselves into existence—but a beautiful transformation is happening as we hold back, keep silent, and receive. We are unlearning. We are unpopular.

THE LETTER OF PROVOCATION ON OUR FACES

Blessed is the gift that we are to the church now. It's silent and inactive. If I were to write a letter to the church, I'd say this: You must listen and look. Our faces are beckoning all the functional assets in the church body. They are a mirror for your own. What do you see? Our weakness is also an authority. Our stripped-down, bare faces summon your vocation to love. A word of God can be received from our faces too, "inscribed" in our otherness, "a double expression of weakness and demand."[11] Look at our vulnerability and ask what it demands of you.

Sure, you are looking into traumatized faces. But I think we need the same thing as everyone else: help to dig out our story. And we need Church folk who will stay in the room when the whole messy story comes out, who will lament with us, and who will help us imagine the joy of *with*ness through it. We want to find freedom in belonging instead of a church fueled by fear and shame. We want to be seen as an invaluable part of the body of Christ, helping others see the whole picture of Christ more clearly. We need someone to help us see Christ in ourselves, which helps us to die to the parts that aren't our real selves. Then we can see the masks we've been wearing as husks that need shedding. We want to be invested in, cared for, invited to contribute where the Spirit directs, and beckoned by your faces.

FOR NOW

For now, we warm the seats with thankfulness that we have held onto the friendships that survived and for the new ones we've made. We wonder how long we will exercise this new nonfunctional asset gift in the church. I think of all the nonfunctional assets whose faces weren't visible to me before. Or those I judged. They did not see their gift or my face in their own, and I did not experience the awakening they were calling me to.

Eleven

FACING GOD'S FACE

A Sermon

Listen! Look![1]

Why is that so hard for us? Every day we're hustling, and we don't even realize it. We strive for our version of the good life, while trying to figure out what is real. Deep down, we want to experience God. Isn't that a big reason we are here? Because we really want to listen. We want to hear him and see him. But, man, it's so hard. It's hard to get out of the habitual self—the one that showered, made breakfast, cleaned breakfast, let the dogs out, peeked at your emails, reviewed social media, overthought your weekend interactions and relationships, got in the car, and rushed to the next thing.

Sometimes Christianity doesn't seem real. I mean, it sounds amazing that God is preparing our souls for love. But it doesn't feel like it most of the time. It feels like I am a mediocre friend, at best, and that I am not doing enough for the church or for my family. I look at my young adult daughters and son and think I haven't taught them or shown them enough about the wonder of who God is and his love for us and I've focused too much on how Christians behave. I catch myself being critical of my husband. I miss him when he's not with me, and then I pick at him when he is. That's not loving. And it feels like I'm always failing in my prayer life.

Not good enough. That seems like real life sometimes. A lot of times.

I know all the right things to respond to how I feel, being a Christian and all. But we each have the winters of our souls to deal with. What I just shared is both embarrassing and dismal. But it is not the worst of my winters. This is the polished confession version.

These changing seasons of the soul are why I love the Song of Songs so much! It is Scripture in condensed form—the whole story before us—told in the best way that we can access it: through poetry, metaphor, typology, and song. The story is told in allegory. And we are able to see the unitive love of Christ for his people, his bride. The woman reveals an unseen realm; she makes visible the invisible. She is typologically pointing us to the city of God, Zion. She stirs our longing for God's presence. This is what's real. God is coming for us.

But, first, a repeated warning. Three times in the Song, the women adjure us not to stir up or awaken love until the proper time.[2] Sometimes we try too hard to force things, and other times we are just dreary and languishing in winter. Our senses are dulled. There's no grass or blooms to smell. We don't hear the birds singing or the voice of children playing outside. We don't feel the sun on our skin. Everything we taste is canned or imported. Likewise, the promises of God can seem so distant or disconnected from real life. They sound great, but right now you are trying to finish your education and start your career before your car breaks down again. Or maybe you are too overwhelmed by the loss of a relationship to sense anything hopeful now. Whether we are caring for loved ones, aching in loneliness, coping with and fighting an illness, just slogging through the mundanity of everyday stresses, or striving to make a record of all our accomplishments and "living" on social media, real life can rob us of curiosity and imagination. When you're going through winter, spring doesn't seem real anymore. But it is. Sunday is coming.

But what if it is exactly curiosity and imagination that need to be awakened to see and sense real life? What if we need reminding to listen and look because spring is rolling in?

> Listen! My love is approaching.
> Look! Here he comes,
> leaping over the mountains,
> bounding over the hills.
> My love is like a gazelle
> or a young stag.
> See, he is standing
> behind our wall,
> gazing through the windows,
> peering through the lattice. (Song 2:8–9)

We begin with exclamations to listen and look. We hear a call to awaken! This passage has seven verbs that her lover does. He is *approaching, coming, leaping, bounding, standing, gazing,* and *peering*. She has one active lover! We can positively say that he is awakening love. And he's doing so in the perfect, complete number of ways—seven! No mountain or hill will deter him. Our woman compares her love to a gazelle—better yet, a young stag. Before, she was languishing in lovesickness and the whole scenery changes to answer that call. He is coming for her!

And yet it's interesting as she first depicts this man as leaping and bounding to get to her, and then it seems, as he gets closer, his demeanor changes to standing, gazing, and peering. Virility gives way to tenderness in her presence. And he pleads with her. He tells her about real life.

This young stag is gentle with her as he beckons the woman to arise and come away with him, bookending his invitation with these words. Let's look at how he does this and what it tells us about real life.

WHAT HE CALLS HER

My love calls to me:
Arise, my darling.
Come away, my beautiful one.
For now the winter is past;
the rain has ended and gone away.
The blossoms appear in the countryside.
The time of singing has come,
and the turtledove's cooing is heard in our land.
The fig tree ripens its figs;
the blossoming vines give off their fragrance.
Arise, my darling.
Come away, my beautiful one. (Song 2:10–13)

He calls her *my*. These two letters put together convey a personal, exclusive belonging. The woman says it too: "*My* love is approaching. . . . *My* love is like a gazelle. . . . *My* love calls to me." And he just loves to call her "*my* darling."

These are the fourth and fifth times he addresses her with the endearment *darling*. The other instance this term is used in Scripture is in Judges 11:37, when Jephthah's daughter asks to weep with her *friends* in the mountains for two months before facing her fate. Her darlings are the ones who will wander and weep with her, the ones who will arise and enter into real life with her.

Darling is translated from a Hebrew word that refers to a female companion in particular. But his darling is more than representative of all that is female. He calls her "my beautiful one." She is his beautiful one, his gift, and now he is going to reveal to her that spring and all its beauty is here. The winter is past. Do you see it?

She's also his dove. The dove is a symbol of the Spirit descending upon her, like the dove pictured at the baptism of Jesus and the dove bringing the olive branch to Noah after the flood.[3] This address is a reminder that his Spirit is within her. And it is why he can call her *my*. This man and woman picture a unitive love of Christ and his people. He's already spoken all three of these endearments to her earlier. They seem to build in meaning as he addresses her here: *my darling, my beautiful one, my dove*. The Bridegroom recognizes her, and us, as his gift from the Father to the Son in eternity. We get to covenantally participate in the Father's great love for the Son by the Spirit. And the glory of the triune God is manifest in this. This is real life.

AWAKENING

The man is awakening love. He invites her into the beauty of spring, beckoning her to action. It's time. "Arise," he says.

"Come away," he says. And then he describes spring in bloom because their love is in bloom. Nature tells the story. Can you see the blossoms appearing on the countryside? Can you hear the turtledoves cooing in *our* land? Can you taste the ripening figs? Can you smell the fragrance of the blossoming vines? All of our senses are aroused with this invitation, giving us the sense that her very arising is part of this springtime. He wants to see her, to hear her, to taste her, to smell her. It's their land, their love to share together. And he is awakening her to see it.

This language evokes God's promise of restoration to Israel. It's the language of Zion. There are multiple echoes with the Song in Isaiah 35,[4] and we see several in verse 2: "[The land] will blossom abundantly and will also rejoice with joy and singing. The glory of Lebanon will be given to it, the splendor of Carmel and Sharon, . . . the splendor of our God." We see echoes of abundant blossoming and singing. In the Song, there are echoes regarding Lebanon, which is temple language, and splendor.[5] Maybe you also recognize that earlier in the Song, the woman identified herself as a wildflower of Sharon (2:1). Her splendor is his splendor. And all this blossoming, singing, springtime language reminds us of God's promises to restore the land, restore his people.

These verses are known as Solomon's marriage invitation to the Shulammite, and they also contain a gospel invitation. Solomon means shalom, peace, rest. *Come away* is an invitation to *come to* the true man of rest, the true Solomon. The gospel call is a marriage invitation. And it's an invitation to be "co-heirs of the promised land and fellow members of Israel, the people of God."[6] "In *our* land." This is how he sees her. How can we not be awakened to that?

WAITING ON HER WORD

And yet the man doesn't do all the talking. That's apparent in the whole Song, which opens and closes with the woman's voice. She leads the discussion throughout. And we have a God who listens. More than that, he draws us out of ourselves. He beckons our voice. Because it takes two voices to be coheirs. Can you even believe it? This is real life!

> My dove, in the clefts of the rock,
> in the crevices of the cliff,
> let me see your face,
> let me hear your voice;
> for your voice is sweet,
> and your face is lovely. (Song 2:14)

This is one of my favorite verses in the Song. He is so tender with her. And it reminds me of another invitation to rest in Scripture. Remember the conversation between Moses and the Lord when Moses expresses insecurity in his promises (Ex. 33:12–23)? They didn't match what Moses saw in real life. The Lord told Moses to lead his people up, but the Lord hasn't said whom he would send with Moses. He told Moses that he found favor with him, but he hasn't yet taught Moses his ways. The Lord replied, "My presence will go with you, and I will give you rest" (Ex. 33:14). Moses doesn't want to go anywhere without the presence of the Lord. And he has a bold ask: "Please, let me see your glory" (v. 18). The Lord is gracious to give him a glimpse of himself but tells Moses that he cannot see his face, "for humans cannot see me and live" (v. 20). So where does he put Moses? In *the crevice of the rock*, so he is protected. He is able to see the Lord's back as he passes by (Ex. 33:20–23). It was glorious.

Today we get a picture of the appropriate time to fully awaken love through Jesus. The Messiah calls to us, his dove, in the clefts of the rock, the crevices of the cliff, and invites us to see his glory. He is the one requesting, "Let me see your face." Do you see that? We are invited to see his face with our face—and live! Because of Jesus. We're invited into his presence, which will go with us and give us rest. We don't have to look at his back anymore; we can see his face. Real life was too much for us before, but we can look now! He will show us his ways.

We have so much trouble seeing what's real. Here's what's real: your voice is sweet and your face is lovely. Christ pleads, "Let me see it; let me hear it." How absolutely amazing this is! The Bridegroom doesn't just come for his bride and take her because he is a mighty stag or gazelle and so she's his for the taking. He speaks reality, paints the picture, evokes all her senses, woos, coaxes, and sparks her memory with all these echoes of his promises in his Word, so that she knows it's him. He's the One. Therefore, he would never just take. He waits for her voice. He gives.

This all reminds me of a Malcolm Guite poem about the annunciation. He too speaks of what we miss in reality, what we don't or won't or can't see. And he writes about a similar moment, when the angel announces the good news to Mary—and waits for her voice:

> We see so little, stayed on surfaces,
> We calculate the outsides of all things,
> Preoccupied with our own purposes
> We miss the shimmer of the angels' wings.

> They coruscate around us in their joy,
> A swirl of wheels and eyes and wings unfurled;
> They guard the good we purpose to destroy,
> A hidden blaze of glory in God's world.
> But on this day a young girl stopped to see
> With open eyes and heart. She heard the voice—
> The promise of His glory yet to be
> As time stood still for her to make a choice.
> Gabriel knelt and not a feather stirred.
> The Word himself was waiting on her word.[7]

I'm usually just looking at the outside of things. I think of real life as the surfaces before me. I get caught up in the drama of the day, the tasks before me, and what other people think, and I miss the glory of real life, the glory God is working all around us. The spring that is blossoming even now. I'm usually on the other side of the lattice. Every now and then I get a glimpse of the Lord's back when he passes by.

But he calls us. He reminds us of spring. And he not only comes to us. He says, "My dove." He's already within us. The Lord's presence is with us as he is directing us and transforming us for glory. Still, he waits for our voice as he bids us to speak. Mary listened and looked. She found reality in the face of God, in the face of her son. Yes, Mary was favored and special, like Moses. She was also a young girl—and he waited on her word! We too are favored. The bride of Christ—does it get more favored than that?

What did Mary speak? "'I am the Lord's servant,' said Mary. 'May it happen to me as you have said'" (Luke 1:38). Her consent must have coruscated with the angels' wings, reverberating to heaven, her whole body filled with that joy. Jesus bids us to use our voices to testify about him. Was it not Mary's testimony about this moment that made it into Luke's gospel? How did Luke know these details? He said, "Let me hear your voice." And she said it again.

HELPING ONE ANOTHER SEE

Like the women in the Song, Mary listened and looked. Gregory of Nyssa referred to the bride in the Song as the teacher.[8] I couldn't agree more. We need to learn from this woman. She represents us: who we are, where we are headed, and who we want to be there with. She gives us the words to say to God. Isn't that wonderful? I read the Song sometimes and think, "Oh wow, I can talk to God like this?" She is so bold, immodest, and blunt. She speaks her insecurities and fears, names her abuse. She asks him where in the world he is right now. She makes her requests, showing us how to cultivate our desires. And she testifies to us, telling us what kind of man our Savior is. We need to learn from her.

In this scene, she stops to see. She heard the voice. She tells us, "Listen! Look!" Esther Meek calls beauty "an event to which you are summoned to show up."[9] We are being summoned to show up to real life. But the bride is telling us that we have to stop looking at the outside of things. We even do this in church. We parse careful theological statements and miss the love and dynamism behind them. We state propositions about God, but we don't see. We are preoccupied with our own purposes, and we miss the shimmer of the angels' wings scintillating around us in their joy. We need to look and listen like the bride and like Mary. And we need our brothers and sisters to remind us to do this. We need summoned back to reality. Out of the cliffs of the rock. Out of fear. Out of shame. Things are not as they seem.

Do you see the glory ascribed to the woman? To you, me, the church? We help one another see. We make Christ's love visible. We remind his people where we are headed.

We are being summoned to know Christ and all he has to show us—beautiful reality.

It's so easy to get caught up in the striving: for a good reputation, approval, attention, companionship, success, children that turn out well, or maybe to get through the day without losing it on someone. What are you striving for? What does that reveal about what you value? What story do you tell yourself about who God is and what he wants from you? When have you experienced the love of God or felt his nearness? Here is the challenge for when we are caught up in the hustle: sit for a minute in the Lord's presence and listen and look for reality. Look for Christ in the faces around us. Be curious. Feel your breath and take in the gift of the moment. Come out of the clefts of the rock and position yourself face-to-face with God. Like the bride, remind one another to listen and look, to testify to God's presence, and to help point others to it. Encourage one another with the words of Christ: "Let me see your face. Let me hear your voice. For your face is lovely and your voice is sweet."

Part Four

THE NAKED
FACE

Twelve

LOOKING FOR MARKS OF HIS GLORY IN ONE ANOTHER

Matt and I stayed overnight in Annapolis, Maryland. We were attending a regional meeting of the Presbytery of the Mid Atlantic for the Orthodox Presbyterian Church (OPC) nearby the next morning, May 1, 2021. This overnight excursion was meant to help with my nerves because I was using the "proper church channels" to address harm done to me locally and more broadly in my denomination. Matt and I would be unable to speak at this meeting, but we were attending to support my elders and pastor. And I wanted my presence to make a statement: these elders and pastor are defending a *real person*. That's why they were there. Ecclesial (a fancy word for "church") charges were filed against them for the way they addressed the offending party. The question was, who are the real victims in all of this? Yes, I realize how cockamamie this all sounds as I'm writing it.

Matt and I were still on a bit of a high from our evening in Annapolis, soaking up every minute that morning before leaving the hotel. We were not ready to switch into church-business mode. Even after all the craziness we'd endured in the church already, we were naive enough to think this would be a reasonable meeting. The presbytery is made up of pastors and elders from around our region. We hoped that our church, and maybe even eventually I, would begin to receive some care and direction. We drove up to a very small church located in a trailer for the meeting. There we were, all together. Compact. Barely a year after the COVID-19 outbreak. No one was wearing a mask. We awkwardly hunted for a seat. The moderator introduced the chair of the ad hoc committee, who was assuming his position behind the pulpit in a posture to speak authoritatively on behalf of the committee. That's when I couldn't believe my ears.

We don't need to recover from the *Bible*.

He was introducing the nature of the conflict of these charges when he blurted out this tutelage. It was a reference to the title of my book *Recovering from Biblical Manhood and Womanhood*. He was supposed to be explaining the committee report's recommendation regarding the charges filed against most of my elders and my pastor before the presbyters voted on whether those charges were in order. I've learned that there are always committees and recommendations from committees in the Presbyterian world. There was supposed to be another vote after that, an additional committee report regarding an appeal made by a disciplined elder in my church. The charges were filed, and the official documented complaints were filed. We heard the "you didn't do it right" excuse instead of dealing with the actual harm taking place. There were recommendations on how to vote. There were official titles and important meetings filled with white men making all the decisions—in a church that doesn't seem to acknowledge the pandemic. This man was standing up front, speaking authoritatively about proper church order, while also speaking out of order with his own commentary that demeans and misrepresents the woman who was sitting in front of him hoping for justice. Apparently, you could do that if you were the right man.

The title of my book directly addresses a contemporary movement in evangelicalism called Biblical Manhood and Womanhood. You don't have to like the title, but it is not by any means suggesting that we need to recover from the Bible. It is suggesting that just because you put the word *biblical* in front of something doesn't make it so. And using the word *biblical* like that can be quite manipulative and damaging. The title is not for everyone. That's fine. But what I cannot and could not accept was his extra commentary in a presbytery meeting where I had no voice to defend my work. I wasn't the one they were supposed to be making a judgment on. And I had no agency to speak. How was it okay for this presbyter to misrepresent my work with his authoritative voice and poison the well to the whole presbytery? But I had no power to defend it. How was that in order?

As this chair of the committee went on with his recommendation, things got worse. He continued to pepper in personal commentary, minimizing the damage done to me, suggesting that I and the denominational leaders who publicly supported me are troublemakers just like the offenders, calling it "online back and forth." He commented that one group said, "You are disrupting the peace of the church," the other said, "We are upholding the purity of the church," and besides, it wasn't us but *that lady* who was disrupting the peace.

That lady. That's me. I was sitting right there. I was referred to as "that lady" twice.

I have a name. I'm a real person. I thought my presence made that clear. Apparently not. But he continued. Talking about "the online back and forth," he jokingly recommended that all parties get off the internet and take a walk. As if I had that privilege. As if my writing vocation that was being maligned didn't matter. As if I didn't depend on accurate book reviews, online engagement, and a good reputation with my work as an author. As if we all should just ignore church leaders who harass women and let it all go away.

He got a laugh. And I sat there—the real person who has been harmed significantly by one of these groups. I felt invisible. The moderator of the meeting didn't call anything out of order. If I spoke, I'd be out of order. I should have spoken. Matt sat there not knowing if he would make things worse for me or for our pastor and elders if he spoke his mind. Even though he really didn't care if he was out of order. No one spoke. Just the laughs. Elders and pastors laughed at it all. At me. Now we both regret not speaking out of order. At the time, it seemed so unbelievable. So surreal. And he just went on.

The message was clear: *you don't belong here.* It was a message I received continually from my denomination for a year—both from church officers and in presbytery committee reports, meetings, and rulings. But no one pressed any charges against me regarding what I actually did wrong, only backhanded corporate acts.

The title of my book *Recovering from Biblical Manhood*

and Womanhood has become a subtitle for a long stage of my life. It's all so strange. I would get remarks saying something like, "Well, you should expect this kind of stuff if you write about something so controversial." You know, dehumanizing stuff from church officers—expect that. It's the same argument as that joke. Take a walk because it's your fault for being on the silly internet. It's victim blaming.

I had to keep asking myself: What controversial teaching has led to me losing a job, losing friends, and spiritual abuse by church authorities? Was it writing about how women should be invested in and have agency as disciples, as sisters in God's church? Or about how men and women should treat one another not as possible affairs but as unique human beings whom we are responsible to help promote in holiness? Even though my work and I are called ungodly, satanic, Jezebel, and many other lovelies; even though officers in my denomination plotted together to call ahead of my speaking engagements to warn churches to guard their families from me; even though my own shepherding elder at church left me exposed and uninformed; even though denominational leaders collectively strategize to sabotage my Amazon page; even though I am openly reviled on a presbytery floor during a trial without rebuke, called a ruthless wolf, among other accusations—the ad hoc committee for my own presbytery in my own denomination reduced it all in their recommendation report regarding the appeal from my former elder as "coarse critique" from a "Reformed website." That legitimizes their abuse. And I am portrayed in the trope of the unsatisfiable woman.

Yes, it is time for recovery.

I couldn't feel the whole impact of that meeting at the time. In retrospect, it was one of the most traumatizing experiences of my life. It didn't seem real. We sought safety in the church. We sought Christ in their faces. We needed cared for. And we found a bunch of men pretending to be bad lawyers. Matt and I returned to our car completely disillusioned. We came expecting Christlike leadership. We saw with our very own eyes how the Book of Church Order[1] can be debated for three hours, without care for the people, the church, or the leaders. We saw disdain anytime victims were mentioned—or those who defend them. I was given no dignity as a person or a member of the OPC. I was "that lady." And it all proceeded without any reference to Scripture, Christ, or the gospel. And then, time's up—no time to get to that appeal. That will have to be an additional meeting, which means it will not reach this year's General Assembly (the Grand Pooh-Bah, or annual Supreme Court of the OPC) for oversight if desired. That will take over another year. How is a church supposed to continue ministry under this ugliness? The process clobbers the sheep. Man, we regretted not speaking out of order. In the car, Matt said, "What were they going to do, put us in OPC jail?" That's what it all felt like in there. And we saw clearly that only the men in power benefit from my silence.

That debacle drove me to the Song of Songs. Is there a better verse in the Bible than the bride herself saying, "I belong to my beloved, and his desire is for me"? (Song 7:10 NIV). This frees us. What does it free us to? It frees us not to try and be in the same boat of power lust, not to protect some new system, but to give our whole selves in love to him. We are free to serve him. And the woman in the Song reveals

---

1. This is the official book guiding church officers in how the governing bodies of the church work and how to approach and enact church discipline.

that we really are a gift to Christ, from the Father, by the Spirit, in all eternity. We have that dignity of being joyfully received. He gave his life to do so. He is our unremitting advocate at the right hand of the Father, right now.

What I sat under was not real. There is freedom in belonging, freedom to love, freedom to give, freedom not to be ensnared in these cages of devaluing and dismissal. We know our value. And our presence is celebrated by our beloved.

BAREFACED

I went to that presbytery meeting seeking oversight, protection, and care, only to be mocked by church officers. They did not see the vulnerable face before them; they saw a threat to their image and power. I was struggling to find Christ in that room. And yet I'm called to listen and look for Jesus. But how do we move forward from this? What kind of leaders do we need? We need leaders who see what Christ sees, who give us keys and not cages, and who aren't led by fear, don't enable harm, and can hold and tend to our wounds. Jesus isn't afraid of our pain, and his body shouldn't be either. As Grace Hamman puts it, "In the passion, if we truly look at the face of Jesus, we come unavoidably face-to-face with human pain."[1] Jesus enters our wounds. We need leaders to help us understand that if Christ is united to his church, then we are all connected.

We need barefaced leaders. And that takes a lot of bravery and emotional and spiritual maturity. When we look past the visage of a face, past the masked story it tells, to see "the naked face,"[2] we can see what God sees. In being attuned to others, we can see their fractures and their wounds. And that brings out our own wounds. As the body of Christ, we are connected in this way. And he is connected to us in this way. Because of this, we look for marks of his glory in one another. Richard Rohr explains, "God has been trying through all of history to give away God."[3] My otherness in that meeting was a provocation for the church leaders to see the Lord and his goodness. What was foggy for us in the meeting became clear when Matt and I got in the car. Everyone was wearing a mask. And we were expected to wear one as well.

Emmanuel Levinas speaks of how, when our faces meet, we are both facing and defacing one another.[4] We notice the attributes of a face and see its welcoming or lack thereof, but to really get to the holiness and the humanness of a face, we need to get behind its countenance to the naked face. Defacement is this getting behind what is presented on the face to see the person in the raw. Levinas asks:

> What does the face say when I approach it? This face, exposed to my gaze, is disarmed. Whatever countenance it then takes on, whether this face belongs to an important person, accompanied by some pedigree, or a person more simple in appearance, the face is the same—exposed in its nudity. From beneath the countenance it gives itself, all its weakness pierces through and at the same time its mortality, to such an extent that I may wish to liquidate it completely.[5]

Isn't that powerful? And scary? At that meeting, my face was liquidated. I felt those words. They were arrows. And yet God calls us to be barefaced, to be introduced to ourselves in a sense—the self we've been covering up, compensating for, and reinventing. He wants to resurrect that raw self in all its glory. And in a sense, he wants us to join in the Spirit's work of resurrecting all the other selves around us by seeing his beauty and holiness in their naked faces. We are to draw out one another's bare faces and honor them. In this act, I believe we all become more real. I am drawing out what is unique to you, which also draws out what's unique in me.

And it can make us feel so vulnerable because we see one another's wounds exposed with bare faces—fears, humiliations, and shame that keep us stuck and stunted. We avoid that gaze and try to represent a better version of ourselves. In our face-to-face encounters, during which our right brains are working in turbo time for that mind matching, we have the intuition to catch that bareface before us and connect with it. You can only see it for its beauty and holiness with your own bareface.

The term *bareface* has a keen history. It seems that even the great C. S. Lewis couldn't always get the original titles he wanted for his books. That makes me feel better. Originally, he pitched *Till We Have Faces* with the title *Bareface*, and his editor Jocelyn Gibb shot it down. In defending *Bareface*, he wrote to her on February 16, 1956, saying he thought readers would be intrigued by its cryptic nature, putting the juice of his argument in parentheses: "(The point, of course, is that Orual after going bareface in her youth, is made really and spiritually bareface, to herself and all the dead, at the end)."[6] Isn't that the story of many of our lives? By February 29, he wrote to Gibb again with his new title suggestion, taken from the line at the end of his book that we looked at in the preface with Orual's vision before the gods:

The complaint was the answer. To have heard myself making it was to be answered. Lightly men talk of saying what they mean. Often when he was teaching me to write in Greek the Fox would say, "Child, to say the very thing you really mean, the whole of it, nothing more or nothing less or other than what you really mean; that's the whole art and joy of words." A glib saying. When the time comes to you at which you will be forced at last to utter the speech which has lain at the center of your soul for years, which you have, all that time, idiot-like, been saying over and over, you'll not talk about the joy of words. I saw well why the gods do not speak to us openly, nor let us answer. Till that word can be dug out of us, why should they hear the babble that we think we mean? How can they meet us face to face till we have faces?[7]

Bareface, the naked face, till we have faces—maybe this is all still sounding too abstract to you. What are we getting at? It is an abstract concept. I love the world of the abstract, but not all do. Even after Lewis published his book, some readers still asked about the meaning Lewis was getting at in his title, *Till We Have Faces*. This is how he replied to Dorothea Conybeare when she asked:

How can they (i.e. the gods) meet us face to face till we have faces? The idea was that a human being must become real before it can expect to receive any message from the superhuman; that is, it must be speaking with its own voice (not one of its borrowed voices), expressing its actual desires (not what it imagines that it desires), being for good or ill itself, not any mask, veil, or *persona*.[8]

We can go our whole lives and not get to our bareface, never freeing ourselves to listen to our own voice or express that real ache inside of us. What lies in the center of our souls that needs cultivating while we are too busy with all the other things we believe we should desire? What do we say idiot-like over and over? It's so hard to get to the center, and many people are just plain terrified of it. Do we listen to the information our wounds are giving us? Lewis's novel brings all this out, teaching us in ways doctrine cannot. Art can do that.

Artists are usually great unmaskers. Bestselling author, poet, songwriter, filmmaker, and playwright Julia Cameron writes, "Making a piece of art may feel a lot like telling a family secret." In this making, what we value, as well as our fears, humiliations, and shame, are revealed. "The act of making art exposes a society to itself."[9] This exposure is confrontational. It makes us look at our masks in all their distortions. It's a bringing-to-light. But many want to remain in darkness.

Darkness is what I felt in that presbytery meeting. My writing exposed something and asked for something that wasn't acceptable to them. Writing is a form of art. And it's an act of hope. Hope is disruptive. Hope makes us look at our current conditions and see how turned the wrong way they are. Hope says, "Rise up." In that invitation, our longings are beckoned, but we also see our weakness. We cannot rise up alone. Do we keep wearing these death masks, which are like tombs for unlived lives, or do we look for Christ? He sends himself. Are we brave enough to search for him?

FINDING MARKS OF HIS GLORY IN OUR WOUNDS

Orual thought she was brave—until her veil was ripped off and she was bareface before the gods. Before, she thought they had no answer. But after her vision, she wrote, "I know now, Lord, why you utter no answer. You are yourself the answer."[10] Our life's work is to shed the veil we put on. We need to shut up that inner critic, whose voice distracts us from the whispers of the Spirit. Deep at the center of our souls we long to experience God. But seeing God's face terrifies us. We will truly be barefaced, exposed, called out of the clefts of the rock. But this encounter brings beautiful clarity. Minister and author Howard Thurman stressed the importance of coming face-to-face with God:

> The central fact in religious experience is the awareness of meeting God. The descriptive words are varied: sometimes it is called an encounter; sometimes, a confrontation; and sometimes, a sense of Presence. What is insisted upon, however, . . . [is that] the individual is seen as being exposed to direct knowledge of ultimate meaning . . . in which all that the individual is, becomes clear as immediate and often distinct revelation. He is face to face with something which is so much more, and so much more inclusive, than all of his awareness of himself that for him, in the moment, there are no questions. Without asking, somehow he knows.
>
> The mind apprehends the whole—the experience is beyond or inclusive of the discursive. . . . The individual in the experience seems to come into possession of what he has known as being true all along. The thing that is new is the realization. And this is of profound importance.[11]

How many times have you had this experience? None? One? Maybe you've had micro-experiences? We can find marks of this knowing in the encounters we have with others. Often it is not in expected ways. We don't expect it to be in the wounds we are trying to hide. The ones we are working not to expose.

October 2, 2023

Here we go again. . . . I knew sharing about Katie preaching with her baby strapped to her chest on my Substack would provoke my haters. The "I told you sos" would pour down like rain. "Aimee going to a church with a woman pastor." I wrote Katie about the piece before I posted it, asking if she was comfortable with me sharing it. It described such a beautiful, transformative picture and moment for me. And here we are again. Some "journalist" wrote an article about me being an apostate, an abomination to God, Jezebel, blah, blah, blah. Whatever. Get some new material. That isn't the bad part. This woman went digging to figure out what church this was. I didn't name the church in my Substack newsletter for a reason. Why bring the vitriol against me to them? She sleuthed the internet, found the Methodist church near me, and then copied and pasted pictures of Katie and her children from the worship service onto her hit piece! Lord, why? Who does this? Here I am again, bringing trouble to a church. All of that trauma is surfacing again. I'm going to have to tell Katie. I need to build up the courage to do that.

I did not want to tell Katie. "Here, look at all the ugliness I bring to your church and to your precious kids!" I felt so protective and mad for them. This "journalist" painted Katie as a horrible mother, as a wicked woman, and next to this hatred are the faces of her beautiful boys. But I know these kids are being shown the love of Jesus. Thinking about that calmed me some. I wished this "journalist" and the astonishing number of people sharing her post knew that love too. Christ's blood was shed for us. And he is with us.

They cannot take that. I hope they can accept a spot at the table too. I wish they could see it.

But I was still working up the courage to tell her as I drove my son back to college that Monday morning. That's when the text came from Katie. Her colleague saw it on social media. And Katie was checking in to see how I was doing. She told me she talked to one of the church's lay ministers, just in case they need to handle some internet trolls, and asked the lay minister to pray for me and for her too. Then Katie shared something the lay minister said: that if I'm hurting, they're all hurting, because that's what it means to be the church. That was incredibly meaningful to hear. I don't know this lay minister. Or anyone, really. But I can tell you this, it was a completely different experience than I received from my former denomination. I never heard that. My wounds were exposed, and Christ revealed himself in them. These leaders saw him there.

> . . . for Christ plays in ten thousand places,
> Lovely in limbs, and lovely in eyes not his
> To the Father through the features of men's faces.
> —*Gerard Manley Hopkins*[12]

Thirteen

WHAT THE FACE
DEMANDS

Her mom was such a fabulous mystery.

Beautiful—the kind of attractiveness that everyone talks about. The young and old, especially her friends, reminded her that her mother was stunning.

Confident—this quality attracted friends. She seemed to know something that the insecure moms didn't. She's figured it out and they wanted in on it. She gave away smiles so freely, the real kind that said *I'm glad to see you.*

Curious—she had a hunger for life. She let herself wonder and wrote songs or painted pieces about it. It all became a work of art. She *was* a work of art.

Brave—she always went for it. It's what everyone envied and hated about her.

Independent—this was the paradox. She married at sixteen, three months pregnant. Love was her ticket to freedom. There wasn't the option to pursue higher education. Wearing blue jeans, playing cards, listening to secular music, and going to prom were her expressions of resistance and rebellion against the fundamentalist-Baptist-preacher tyranny she lived under. This baby was her escape. This was a love story. And everyone saw it that way. Strangers noticed, stopping to tell them how attractive their family was. They enjoyed one another. She loved her family, but she had lost something in the exchange between the family she escaped and the one she was trying to build. Something she never quite had—that's what she needed to find.

The ticket to her freedom was now fourteen, looking out the family room window, impatient and mad. She is beginning to learn of the power and vulnerability of being a woman. I wonder what I would tell her now. If I could stand behind her and put my hand on her fourteen-year-old, load-bearing shoulder. She feels it, whatever this restlessness is in her mom. She feels her mom pulling away. And she is mad. She knows her mom got off work an hour ago. Why is *she* the one dealing with her brother and sister? Why isn't her mom here with her family? She should be the one having fun with her friends, not her mom.

It runs deeper than that though. That is the shallow layer of her anger. Deep down, she wants her mom to show more interest in her, like she used to. Now, when she looks at her mom, it feels like her mom is not there, not present, not seeing her. And fourteen-year-olds have a lot of shit to figure out. She too used to feel beautiful, confident, curious, brave, and independent. Now she feels so fragile.

I think I would tell this fourteen-year-old that this is a strange thing, a curious one, if she would allow herself to think about it. In a sense, she and her mom are both fourteen-year-olds, although in different dimensions. With her youngest sister now seven, her mom is at a point in her life where she is again faced with herself. She too is seeing just how fragile her beauty, confidence, curiosity in life, bravery, and independence are. She too is entering new friend circles that aren't centered around mothering children (or being children) and that are drawing desires out of her to learn more about what she loves, what she fears, and what she wants to do in life. The trauma of her own childhood and her daring, loving escape have left her stunted. Something in her didn't get to develop fully. But all this time her beauty, magnetism, and love for her family masked it so damn well. And maybe she resented the man she married and loved for the way she felt infantilized by it all.

"Your fears are right," I'd tell her. "She is going to leave. It will mess with your sense of self and your own questions about being a woman—fiercely. You'll let yourself be vulnerable and beg her to stay. You'll stoop to trying to emotionally manipulate her. Then you will hate her. You weren't enough for her to stay.

"That mom you thought you had has to die. She's not that person anymore. That was part of the mask.

"It has nothing to do with your value. Both of you are going to fall on your faces trying to figure it all out. But you find one another again—your truer selves. You will see each other and come to wonder in the stories your faces tell to one another. And the beauty is more glorious with the scars, the confidence is set in humility, the curiosity is more thrilling than ever, and the bravery is more honest about fear. You will loosen your grip on the invisible cages of independence and exchange that for the gift of freedom in belonging."

That fourteen-year-old is me.

THE COMMANDMENT OF THE NAKED FACE

Bareface is vulnerable. Even going back to this memory, as a mature adult woman, telling it from the perspective of my present self speaking to my fourteen-year-old self, is incredibly emotional work. Every now and then, I would get a flash of that memory and the anger and anxiety I felt looking out that window. I found it triggered early in my marriage when my husband was late coming home from work (and he, like my mom, sees time as more of a suggestion). I would panic a little. So I did some work, considering why I was afraid and anxious and connecting a few of the dots. But it wasn't until recently that I tapped into the raw feelings behind my fear. I revisited that young girl and let myself feel all of it again. The funny thing is, letting myself see my own naked face and being exposed to those wounds and feelings again didn't cause the anger and anxiety that my flash memory used to trigger. I felt compassion not only for myself but for my mom. Don't get me wrong, I cried. I let myself be sad and experience that loss. But I saw her differently from where I am now. It helps that I've had many years afterward of Mom looking at my face with that same grace. But we went through our junk to get to that point.

When we look at the naked face of the other—even if that other is our raw self—it demands something of us. We are in a sense looking at the holiness and vulnerability of that person. They are exposed. But that same weakness is also an authority.[1] The naked face of the other summons our vocation to love. Emmanuel Levinas nailed it when he said that to see a nude face is to see its weakness, giving us the power to liquidate[2] it completely if we desire. We see the wounds and can exploit them. We hold the power to humiliate, shame, neglect—or to sabotage our selves. But this weakness, this "possibility of murder," is accompanied by a command. The "face is the site of the word of God." And what is that word? It's very recognizable to us: "Thou shalt not kill." And all that is implied with it—namely, the greatest commandment of all, to love. Behold the power of the face, which "is wholly weakness and wholly authority."[3] As the title of the book of interviews with Emmanuel Levinas, which has so deeply influenced my meditations on the face, asks: *Is It Righteous to Be?* Yes. Our faces summon the humanity of the other. They summon us to life!

When I first wrote this memory, it was between me and my journal. And that is where I intended it to stay. I didn't want to expose this bareface to my mom. While I thought about the growth that could come from it, I knew how uncomfortable it would be. Would it be too painful for her to read? I convinced myself that I was protecting her by keeping it to myself. When the idea for this book was conceived, I was faced with different questions. Who am I to make that decision on her behalf? Do I want to withhold an opportunity for my strong mother to see my growth and my ability to see her with understanding, based on my poor judgment of her fragility? Maybe my fear is what's preventing me. So often, we rob others and ourselves of the blessings and healing God is ready to give us when we are unwilling to be vulnerable. We don't want to be barefaced because it's scary to acknowledge the weakness and authority of that command, "Thou shalt not kill." What if we are liquidated? And we too often miss looking into the bareface of the other because we do not want to behold the holiness and vulnerability that calls us to an obedience to love. Love me, your neighbor, as yourself. Love yourself as you are loved by Christ.

In planning for this book, I knew there would be some memories like this one that needed to be in it. How can I let the private thoughts in my journal be put into print? Under my recollection of this memory in my journal, I wrote a verse I'm often in conversation with, John 12:24: "Truly I tell you, unless a grain of wheat falls to the ground and dies, it remains by itself. But if it dies, it produces much fruit." Think about the juxtaposition between this saying of Jesus and the command "Thou shalt not kill." We should nurture what is alive. But part of that is recognizing what takes from a fruit-bearing life. What needs to die because it is striving to glorify our egos and personification of self? Fourteen-year-old Aimee needed to die to her expectations, righteousness, and demands. She even had to die to good things, like wanting her family to stay together, security, and attunement. I want to bless her longings to be like her mother as well as her confusion when the same qualities turned her bitter for so long. Bless her pain as she dies to the idea that she needs to be enough. Put it all in the ground and let Christ do his work. This forty-eight-year-old woman needs to die to her fears—of exposure, vulnerability, how she is going to be perceived, and of wounding her mom—to allow herself the opportunity to validate and hold this memory with her mom. We need to go back in time for both our sakes and rewire the way we tell our story. That's powerful. That's the work I am inviting you to in this book. Here I am, hoping my stories provoke your own, and hoping my face makes a demand to find yours.

A CRACK IN HER COUNTENANCE

In making this decision, I knew I would have to have some conversations to honor those well whom I've shared stories about. I had to bring it to them first.[1] I was anxious about these soon-to-be-had conversations—and also so grateful. Not everyone is in a position where it would be healthy to share their memory work with the people in those difficult memories. I still think that the work is important, and that it shouldn't remain isolated. It can be fruitful to share with a therapist or trusted friend. But before I got this far, just narrating the memory like I did tilled up a desire to talk to my mom about it.

February 27, 2023

Two Mondays ago, my mom was here for dinner. I decided to be more curious about her relationship with my grandma and my grandma's history. As I am learning to tell my own story, I need to learn more.

My grandma is the youngest of ten. She is close to her brother, number nine. There is abuse in the family, some that has come to the surface, and much that is still unknown except to those directly affected. My grandma is a look-the-other-way kind of woman. She doesn't dignify any victims by believing them, much less advocating for them. And who knows what her life was like. I know the times were different. But I resent her for it. And our relationship is basically one of small talk if we see one another.

---

1. The irony is not lost on me that I wrote a whole book of context in order to do this. What can I say, this is how authors think!

There are stories behind everything, and we will probably never know them. The work of confronting generational pain helps us understand the command to love, not kill, and apply it in our homes and churches. Who my grandma is has affected my mom. And me. So I started asking some questions over dinner about how my grandma grew up. I learned that her father died while her mom was pregnant with her. That she was the "adored" youngest sibling who always got her way.

I wondered why we knew so little about her. Was she shielded from the abuse around her? If so, how did she become so cold? Was she a victim?

Something loosened in this conversation. I think my curiosity did something to my mom. She shared with me that she never felt loved by her mother. I sort of knew this. Over the years, mom talked about how her mother was with them. She was a rigid, legalistic woman. She weaponized faith. But this is really something to say. It revealed Mom's longing for her mother's love. As we walked from the table and into the kitchen, Mom paused in reflection. And then she said that she knows she's been numb to some things in her life, as a way to cope. This was a huge gift to me. She has no idea. The naming. The recognizing. It was so much to hold. It was so vulnerable that I didn't feel like I could unpack it anymore with her. Just hold it. Recognize it, but not out loud. Just between our faces.

She was so brave to say it.

I wonder if she's thought about it again.

Fourteen

DISCOVERING THE DEATH OF THE OTHER

'm not who you think I am.

I see your pain and your desperation to keep her. And it resonates with me. I want to soothe you and to be there for you in your loneliness and fear. It's going to be okay. We are going to be okay. I will listen to the secrets of your marriage. Some of them fuel my hatred for her. We both use that to try and help us get over her. She's bad; we're good.

But we are both lying to ourselves. It's not that simple. And I am way too fragile to handle all this information. All this pain from my father. My strong father who beat death itself just five years ago.

You need me though, especially when you are over-whelmed by the urge for revenge. You want to make all of her new friends pay—and him in particular, the one who is stealing her heart from us. From you. I will talk you down. I'll remind you that your fantasies for revenge are not really you. You're not really that person.

And this isn't really me. I'm just a teenager, not the mature adult you need, not the pastor or therapist or friend that you need. I try. I'm insightful for my age—thanks to you. But I'm also a wreck. I don't want this role anymore. I want to step into lighter spaces.

I step into those teenage spaces with shame: the shame of the family she left, the shame of the daughter who wasn't enough to keep her, the shame of being a statistic.

So I fake it. I pretend like I don't care. I'm better than her. I look to excelling in the stereotypes of my sex to make me feel like the ideal woman. Cheerleader. Popular. Boyfriends. Look at me and how much I matter. Look at me. (But not too closely.)

I'm not who you think I am. I'm not as strong. It's all quite pathetic, really. It turns out, I'm shallow. I can only handle the shallow end of life right now. When you find your new wife, I'm happy for you. I like her too. But I now must deal with the shift of my role from confidant back to child. You snap back into parent mode and see me spiraling.

I bring you more shame. Just like mom, I'm not who you think I am.

You're gonna have to let me figure it out. I can't stay in the in-between. One marriage, one family, is breaking, and two new ones are being built. I want what was promised before all this: the "you get good grades and go to college" transaction. I won't escape with a pregnancy like she did. I will do it with an education. I'll get the loans. I'll be the first in the family to enter the world of the university and the lifestyle that comes with it. I don't even need you guys.

I'm not who I think I am. No matter how many times I say it. I'm terrified and determined, which is not a great combination. And I'm alone. So alone. Do I have what it takes to follow through? Maybe I can redeem myself in the end and make everyone proud.

Isn't this the same thing you were trying to do? Now I see that you too were striving to rewrite your family story—a version that didn't include your father's alcoholism, abuse, and pissing on your homework. I see how you were trying to reconcile that man with the love he also gave. It was all so hard to make sense of, that the triangulation from your mother felt right. You needed one another to feel sane. How can you reconcile being so grateful for her love and attunement over her whole life with the competition that it made in your marriage? How do you get to the bareface of the boy and man who needed to breathe deeply a fragrance that wasn't the smell of your mother's needs and your father's failures? How do you be a husband and parent without all that pressure to rewrite the whole damn thing?

Who are we when we are done proving we aren't our father or our mother? Who are we when we realize what we've been running from is still tied to our leg and what we were striving for is an illusion? We're not who we thought we were. Thank God for that.

We're making it out of the house of mirrors as we find our faces. I see in your face now mourning for the death of what wasn't, gratitude for the seeds of what is, attunement to and wonder in the mystery of it all, and hope to keep writing the story.

WE DIED

I am learning something powerful about life, family, and church. I've spent most of my adult life worshiping in a tradition that emphasized the need for the church to reform. It claims that it reformed the church amid Roman Catholic abuses and is always reforming to the Word of God. Except it isn't always reforming. It just says that. They are deeply tied to their systems and also blinded by them. But we need more than reform. We need resurrection, and not just that one consummate time when Christ returns—as glorious as that will be and as much as we are anchored in that hope. We also need continual resurrections. It's why that grain of wheat picture Jesus gave us recorded in John 12:24 is so powerful. We set our minds and lives on too many things that try to take life on their own. So much so, that we lose sight of our own faces, each other's faces, and the face of Christ.

I put two verses from Scripture under my journal entry when I did this story work about me and my dad after mom left:

For now we see only a reflection as in a mirror; then we shall see face to face. Now I know in part; then I shall know fully, even as I am fully known. (1 Cor. 13:12 NIV)

For you died, and your life is hidden with Christ in God. (Col. 3:3)

This memory work brings them together in my mind. They also carry an echo of that flailing grain of wheat, while provoking the great mystery of being hidden in Christ and fully known. The trauma of divorce, of being left by a spouse or a parent, causes one to look in the mirror. So does trauma from spiritual abuse. But in our fog, we can't see what we're looking at.

This thought is dark and yet ever before us: the death

of the other. Death represents complete vulnerability and defenselessness. We are terrified of death, so we cover over ourselves and each other with our striving and portrait making. We cover over ourselves because we want to appear competent, pretend we have it together, and seem like we've gotten somewhere in this life and can handle it. And we cover for the other because of the responsibility it calls us to. But it's in the discovery of this death, where we think our end is, that we are invited to join in the resurrection power of Jesus. What a mystery that we cannot write, predict, or control. But what a glory to face and wait in together. We're in a liminal space, where dying and living mingle together. And so I had to die to who I thought my dad thought I was and how I disappointed him. She's not who he needed anyway. He needed the real me, who was full of teenage angst, anxiety, and sadness. The real me provoked his own death to the man that was married to my mom. In discovering each other's death, we dug out our own hiddenness.

We will die, we did die, and each day we are called to die little deaths that don't feel so little at first. Christ meets us in this liminal space. So often, when you ask God to give you what's real, you have a hard time seeing it because you still have a lot of work to do in shedding all your faux securities and certainties. There's so much unreality and pretense within our own selves. It turns out, our cisterns are full of fears, misplaced desires, and self-betrayal. Some deaths are so hard to release to the ground. They are relationships with people you love and care about, but ones that continue to ask you to mask yourself. Seeing your bareface demands others reveal their own, and sometimes they can't bear it. Sometimes when you say, "I'm not who you think I am," they don't want to recognize the you that is coming out of hiding.

FRIENDSHIP DEATH

"Don't show us your face."

This is the message I heard when I began to be able to unearth my pain. I had just begun to examine my pain, put it into words, and lovingly confront those who wanted to be the heroes of my story of harm in the church. But those who saw themselves as helpers also felt the cost. They needed their own hero narrative. But they couldn't look at my face.

They said things like, "I see the trauma in your words. Now is not a good time for you to speak." Or "I wanted to say this to you but felt like I couldn't because of your trauma."

Whatever you do, Aimee, don't let them see your trauma. Trauma is the absence of empathetic witness from the people who are supposed to care.[1] And these were the people who were supposed to care. They needed to be known to others and themselves as people who care. But they cannot handle their own trauma stories, so they cast themselves as these strong characters. They are fragile as can be. They can't look at my whole face, especially the part where they caused the pain. They tried to manage my voice, and they kept speaking for me. They also talked about me—behind closed, masculine doors—to keep their own masks from falling off.

Whatever you do, Aimee, we need to see you as the fragile one. We can't confront your face like a real person we respect because of your trauma. Yes, if I am the fragile one, you remain the protector. You are the decider of what information I can handle, the interpreter of my words. You get to decide that it is my trauma speaking. Therefore, it is not to be taken as logical. And you are above that. Look at your constraint in telling me what you really think so that I won't have a breakdown of some sort.

Do you think I'm too direct, crossing the line, abrasive, insatiable, not letting go, not letting you go back to the way you like to tell it?

Here's your face, Aimee. We've made it for you. And we can't bear to look at you without it.

BLESSING THE LIMINAL SPACE

Liminal space is that time when the grain of wheat is falling to the ground. How hard will the landing be? Who will catch me? It is that space of the tomb of the death. Who will be there with me? How long will it take for resurrection? What will I look like? Do I really believe? Liminal space feels scary and uncomfortable because we are in between. We are not walking through a door of belonging—not even knowing where that door is. And yet there are so many gifts, so many keys dropping all around. Opportunities to receive and give love, receive and give Christ. To notice miracles again. When you hang out near the tombs, you see little resurrections happening everywhere. I will bless this time.

> Blessed are the liminal spaces
> That we didn't ask to be in,
> That force us to look again for a door.
> Look again.
> At our striving,
> Our fears,
> All that we thought we built to be secure.
> Blessed are these transitions,

Even when we don't know what is ahead.
Even when we don't feel secure.
When we are forced to ask what it is we really want,
And afraid to hear our own answers.
Blessed is the waiting,
The developing,
The groaning and grieving of all that we've gotten wrong.
The seventy times seven chances
To participate in goodness.
Blessed is the discovery
Of the raw beauty in the little things,
The freedom to recapture wonder.
To see the glimmer of holiness in a pause,
In an unrehearsed smile,
In a tear not held back.
Blessed are the liminal spaces
That hold us when we cannot find the door of belonging,
And the new world that opens up
As we find liminal inhabitants,
And Christ who meets us there
In their faces.

LOOKING AT THE UNDERGROUND

What if the tomb in the underground[2] is also a mirror where you can see more clearly? The old versions of the stories I told myself are down there, like fallen grains of wheat. Look at it all. What I thought I needed. Who I thought I was supposed to be. My sense of scarcity, shallow markers of identity and success, and my hideous righteous certainty.

Let them decompose. Tell them I have more coming. Each grain of wheat wipes the mirror a little clearer.

I see a new sense of self emerging. *Aimee* means "beloved." This new self has been watered and nurtured in the underground. It's where I began to believe that "I am my love's, and his desire is for me" (Song 7:10). Where I have been hidden in the fullness of all that Christ is and the particularity of how that reflects out of me. Now I'm drawn out in this underground, where I let the unmet expectations on my parents and myself fall off me. And I get to wonder in how grace enables us to see our faces more clearly. What a gift to find my parents down in the underground too. Now our faces provoke one another.

This provocation is "the discovery of the death of the other," as Emmanuel Levinas calls it. The discovery of their "defenselessness, and the nudity of [their] face." The "response to this discovery" provokes our goodness. And it's this discovery that Levinas calls "the face of the other." And he refers to this discovery as "the first language." How strange is this language that has no words but such responsibility. We cover up, stuff down, and look away from this language, yet it "bears thought."[3]

My dad and I share memories quite a bit. As he is reading through this manuscript, he is learning new old things about me. It is provoking his memories and how they've impacted him. I'm learning new parts of my dad's face. We often talk about spiritual mysteries in some of these memories, looking for God's face in the unanswered questions and aches. As I'm writing this chapter arising from complex and painful memories, I'm thinking about our talks and how easy it is for me to be vulnerable with him now. We've been discovering the deaths of each other's faces and responding in goodness. All that I held before, the shame of not being the version I thought he needed—and on some level he thought he needed—is decomposing in the underground.

The pain of divorce doesn't go away for the parents or the children. But Christ meets us in our wounds. The healing creates a scar that testifies. Sometimes we have to go back to those scars, brush our fingers over them, and learn more about how that story is being told. Some lines need cutting, some need reinforcing, some acknowledging, and some lamenting. And new, life-giving lines break through.

The wounds are still open with the many deaths I've died concerning the church. I look in the underground tomb and see things that I can bless—my desires for a sense of belonging, security, purpose, certainty, friendships, what I've given my children, knowing if we will ever join a church again.

December 5, 2023

Katie asked us to light the candle and do the reading this week for the second Sunday of advent. It's our family's first time worshiping in a church with an advent season, the season of waiting. There's so much waiting we will bring with us to the front of the church. In the same week my dear husband, with all his own wounds—ones that he didn't have as much reciprocity and validation to address—is waiting to decide whether it's time for his dad, who is in an advanced stage of dementia, to receive palliative care instead of curative care, to know if we are waiting for him to live or die. Even so, with his dad's dementia, Matt already had to die to many possibilities between them. We will walk up the aisle, waiting for God to show up in this loss.

And we will light a flame while facing the darkness of hearing about another fallen pastor this week. One who made an impact on my life and so many others. One who was distinguished, respected, and apparently cheating on his wife for a decade. How many more? How deep does this go? What is real in church? These questions, these deaths, will walk with us to light the candle of peace this Sunday.

Advent season speaks into the liminal space. The threshold of waiting. And the winter of it all.

One of the most painful lessons is learning how to appreciate the hush of winter, when more growth takes place underground than above ground, and there in quiet, unnoticeable ways.

—*Renita Weems*[4]

Fifteen

HE CAN'T LOOK AT HER FACE

S he escaped once.
We learn this through the voice of a man.

But he came for her "to speak to her heart in order to bring her back" (Judg. 19:3 LSB). What does this speech sound like? We never get to hear it. She never hears it. Or perhaps she did and we aren't privy to it. We do know this: his private expressions of care mean nothing in contrast to the collective harm heaped on her. We see him and her father working out the exchange, spending time together. We see men meeting with men who think and behave like men and who make the decisions to give, take, stay, leave, or sacrifice.

Sacrifice her, not them.

We struggle to find the face of the unnamed concubine in Judges 19. We never hear her voice. We get one glimpse of her agency. Using her last moments of freedom, her last bit of strength, as the light was breaking into the darkness of her nightmare, she makes her way back to the Levite, her master, and collapses at the threshold of his sacral duties.

What has he done? He acquired. He came for her to reclaim her. And he seized her, throwing her out to the wicked men in the city. There he is in full vigor, set to leave alone after sacrificing her body and soul to be ravaged and raped in his place. In his place. All night long. As long as her body can bear it. Now he is forced to look at her. He didn't expect to see her as he opened the door to leave alone that morning. What does her face demand? Metaphorically, she serves at the entrance of the tent of meeting. Look into the bronze basin, Levite, made up of the mirror she reflects back to you. Of who you are, whom you love, and what you will do next.

Now he cannot look at her face.

Is she dead or alive? We do not know. Maybe the language gives us a clue. She is lying at the doorway. *The threshold*. Maybe that's the threshold of life, of what he will do—love or liquidate. Will he be the reaper of revenge, against all but himself?

There she lies. "Get up," he says. "Let's go."

"But there was no response" (v. 28).

Can it get worse? The Levite will now use his carving skills to sacrifice her again. He throws her on his donkey and takes her home, not to be put to rest but to be sacrificed for war and for pride. "When he entered his house, he picked up a knife, took hold of his concubine, cut her into twelve pieces, limb by limb, and then sent her throughout the territory of Israel" (v. 29). Did he send her face? What did he do with it? No matter. There will be war.

In the words of Phyllis Trible:

Of all the characters in scripture, she is the least. Appearing at the beginning and close of a story that rapes her, she is alone in a world of men. Neither the other characters nor the narrator recognizes her humanity. She is property, object, tool, and literary device. Without a name, speech, or power, she has no friends to aid her in life or mourn her in death. Passing her back and forth among themselves, the men of Israel have obliterated her totally. Captured, betrayed, raped, tortured, murdered, dismembered, and scattered—this woman is the most sinned against. In the end, she is no more than the oxen Saul will later cut (*ntḥ*) in pieces and send (*šlḥ*) throughout all the territory of Israel as a call to war (1 Sam. 11:7). Her body has been broken and given to many. Lesser power has no woman than this, that her life is laid down by a man.[1]

How will the Israelites respond?

Trible reveals how we miss the imagery in our English translation when they respond, "Think it over, discuss it, and speak up!" (v. 30). She explains that "strikingly, the first command is actually the Hebrew idiom, 'direct your heart,' followed by the phrase, 'to her.'" Well, this is familiar! "Long ago the man was supposed to speak to the heart of the woman, though he did not. Now Israel must direct its heart to her, take counsel, and speak."[2]

But that is not the response. If we read through the end of this story in Judges 20, the violence against women continues as "the rape of one has become the rape of six hundred." The Israelites swore they would not give away their own daughters as wives to the surviving men of Benjamin's tribe. And they've already killed all the women of Benjamin. So they took four hundred virgins from Jabesh-gilead after murdering all the married women there. But that was still not enough. They took two hundred young women who were dancing at the annual festival in Shiloh. "Israelite males have dismembered the corporate body of Israelite females."[3] Does God approve of this? Are we to condone such violence against women? How can we bear this darkness? Why is it in our Scriptures? I ask you, what do we do with one of the most horrific and evil portions of God's Word?

We must lament it. We should wail over it.

Scripture takes us through this darkness and vile evil carried out by God's so-called people. The coldness of the narrative moves us in outrage and gut-heaving sadness. Do we see what these men wouldn't? Do we feel what these men wouldn't? Can we look at her face? How does that change us? How does that help us look at the faces before us now? What does it draw out of our own faces?

The canon of Scripture directs us to further direct our own hearts to the woman.[4] The Hebrew Bible follows Judges with the story of Hannah (1 Sam. 1:1–2:21), and the Greek Bible follows it with the story of Ruth. Through the telling of the stories of these women during this same time when the judges ruled, we see a different and redemptive narrative. These women are seen, named, revered, and have agency. They give life. The men direct their hearts to them. And this thread of the story leads to Christ, who directs his heart to his bridal people, takes on flesh, and weeps over death—his body, given for many, for the love that burns for her.

Greater love has no man than this.[5]

The unfolding message in Scripture presses us to see what the woman's face reveals.

How we treat our women reveals our eschatological anticipation of joy.

Part Five

THE MATURING FACE

THE LEGACY OF OUR FACES

For years, I thought I disappointed my grandma in my vocations as a coffee shop owner and then a writer. Having grown up through the Great Depression, she wanted us to get stable jobs. She wasn't into taking risks. But both of my parents are. And I really like that about them. When I was growing up, Grams took opportunities in conversation to suggest, "How about you become a dental hygienist?" Then she would tell me about Shirley's granddaughter who went on that path, got the education she needed, and is making good money cleaning teeth. It was such a respectable job in my grandma's eyes, who worked for a dentist as a receptionist for years. The thought of looking into people's mouths all day horrified me, much less working on them. Plus, why didn't she suggest I become a dentist? Grandma was a product of her time, I guess. She did encourage me to get a good education and was very proud of my bachelor of science degree.

Grams didn't tell me not to write. I could just tell that she was nervous about it. She began to warm up as I published my first book. I knew that she was proud. Once, I shared one of my recorded conference talks with my family. My dad told me that when he played it for Grandma, she said something like, "That's one of the best talks I've ever heard in my life." I'm laughing while writing that. It wasn't. But because it was me, she felt that way. Still, even after publishing my first four books, I was insecure about how my grandma thought about me being an author. Some of it was probably just me.

Grandma died in December of 2016. After an unsuccessful surgery to remove a cancerous tumor, she had to stay in a care facility for the little time she had left. I visited her quite a bit, and I saw her get weaker and skinnier with each encounter. She still had her spunk, as long as she could. One of the last visits where Grandma was conscious and conversational is seared into my memory. I didn't realize the impact of it until much later. I kissed my grandma on her forehead to tell her goodbye for the day and was making my way out of the room. She sat up in her bed and firmly called, "Aimee!" I turned to face her. Grandma intently looked me in the eye and pointed her finger at me, "You keep writing. Don't you let them stop you from writing!" It was so strange. I told her, "Okay, Grandma," and smiled before leaving again. But what in the world? Who was going to keep me from writing? I chalked it up to Grandma's many times telling me about her regret of not becoming a nurse and a missionary. Grams had a way of pointing out the patriarchy without using the language. She was faced with an either-or: you have either a family or a career. I think there was a secret feminist in her who never emerged. So I took this as a gift. Grandma's validation and approval—encouragement even—of what I do. It felt good.

Years later, when I was in the thick of spiritual abuse—getting fired from the parachurch organization I worked for,[1] wondering if I even want to keep writing or if it's even worth it, daydreaming about becoming a "beerista"—I remembered. Grandma's words became prophetic to me then. "You keep writing. Don't you let them stop you from writing!" Did she know? My eyes are filling with tears as I'm writing this now. My frail, dying, four-foot-eleven grandma spoke power to truth. I'm a writer. I'm going to hit a hella hornet's nest and doubt will overtake me. They will try to stop me. *Keep writing.* I told Grandma I would.

FINAL BENEDICTIONS

I now look at that face-to-face moment with my grandma as her final benediction to me. What a blessing it was. *Go out from here and give the world yourself, Aimee. Don't stop.* I still have a lot to work through about who that self is. But Grandma, at the end of her life, acted in her vocation as the matriarch of our family, recognizing, affirming, and encouraging the *me* out of me. Looking me dead in the eye until I said it. *Okay.* If I can do that for the people I love and encounter in my life, man, that's the legacy I want: to empower others in the glory they were created for.

Our faces are being formed. At the tail end of my forties, it seems I'm back to the questions I was asking in my early

---

1. Or as they clarified, I wasn't technically fired since they hired me as a contractual worker, and they no longer desired my services.

twenties. What are our expectations of a mature Christian? What does that look like? What do they know? How do they act? Am I one?

The faces we have age and humble us. They remind us of what St. Clare of Assisi revealed about looking into the mirror of eternity and seeing Christ in his poverty, humility, and inexpressible charity. We cannot manufacture this. In a sense, we come to terms with it. It's hard to come to terms with aging, especially in our society where women aren't expected to grow old gracefully. Or at all. It's hard to come to terms with how little of a face I have at this stage in life—with how much I've had to shed because it was put on, not developed. Grandma had a lot to come to terms with at the end of her life. But your death bed brings all this to the surface, and it gives you a special authority. In the most humbling of places, completely vulnerable, we saw her in her poverty, humility, and inexpressible charity. And I walked out with a benediction.

There's a lot of weight given to the deathbed blessings of patriarchs in the Old Testament. So much so, that we have the infamous scene of Rebekah and Jacob scheming to fool Isaac into giving Jacob his elder brother, Esau's, blessing (Gen. 27). And it works. The blessing is so powerful, that when Esau and his father find out, Isaac pretty much says that it's too late and what's done is done. Jacob gets the blessing. When Esau pleads that there must be something left for Isaac to bless him with, his dad doesn't have good news for him. The blessing is a prophecy much harder to swallow than that stew he traded Jacob his birthright for.

When Jacob is close to death, he first blesses Joseph's two sons, the younger given the greater blessing over the older against both custom and Joseph's correction (Gen. 48). He then assembles his twelve sons together, representing the twelve respective tribes of Israel, giving each one "a suitable blessing" (Gen. 49:28), including prophetic words that were not all good (vv. 1–27).

When Joseph dies, he gathers his brothers and prophesies that God is not absent in their darkness. He will visit them and fulfill his word to Abraham, Isaac, and Jacob to bring them to the land of promise. Facing his death, he makes his brothers swear an oath that they will carry his bones from Egypt when this happens (Gen. 50:24–25). There are some interesting Jewish midrashim about how they were recovered. But in Exodus we learn that Moses took Joseph's bones through the wilderness journey, fulfilling this oath. According to the book of Joshua, his bones were buried in Shechem (Josh. 24:32). What a picture of the resurrection! Take my bones with you through the wilderness and plant them in the dirt of the land of the living! In Hebrews, we are told that these deathbed blessings and prophecies were all "by faith" (Heb. 11:20–22).

That coffin traveling through the wilderness with the Israelites and those reburied bones in life-giving dirt symbolized the prenatal blessing of a woman. When Mary visits her cousin in the beginning of her pregnancy, Elizabeth "exclaimed with a loud cry":

> Blessed are you among women, and your child will be blessed! How could this happen to me, that the mother of my Lord should come to me? For you see, when the sound of your greeting reached my ears, the baby leaped for joy inside me. Blessed is she who has believed that the Lord would fulfill what he has spoken to her! (Luke 1:42–45)

Before Jesus's bones rose from the tomb, they were formed in the womb of a young virgin. And before John the Baptist prophesied his arrival,[2] his mom did. Her prenatal benediction was also a sublime deathbed benediction—her Lord's. Blessed are we.

JESUS IS HIDING IN OUR FACES

One of the benefits of being the child of teenage pregnancy is having young parents. Writing this chapter fills me with gratitude in the legacy they've already handed down and all that I hope to still soak in. They both have beautiful faces. Watching them age in their mid-to-late-sixties is such a gift. Their maturing faces are full of great secrets. They reveal the gift of presence. It radiates from them, so that I slow down when we are together. Is there more of a legacy that you can hand down than the power of withness? Isn't this what we long for and miss the most—the gift of being in the room together? Isn't it what we desire from God the most as well? We want to be face-to-face with God so that we can finally see, finally be, and finally see that he sees me. I am blessed to experience some of this presence in the faces of my own parents' attunement. And I believe that in these moments Jesus is hiding in plain sight. *Here I am.*

The maturing faces of my parents also reveal the secret of delight when they light up before the faces of their grandchildren. Legacy multiplying. I wonder sometimes if my kids will remember the younger faces of my parents. When their

---

2. Outside of the womb, anyway. His leaping inside the womb was certainly speaking volumes to his mother!

hair was dark and you couldn't see the lines of their countless smiles and worries. Sure, they have the pictures. But I don't think they want that version of my parents. Many of those smiles and worries were for them—aged in the barrels of grilled cheeses, Band-Aids, pushes on the swing, explorations through the woods, back scratches, storytelling, listening and listening, laughing and laughing, attending their games and events, cheering them on, blowing on the embers of the flames they will become. Now those lines are marked on their faces, radiating before them when their faces meet. How beautiful! You can't tell me Jesus isn't hiding there.

Then there's the big secret of grace. Those mature faces also bear the history of pain. From their own families of origin. From a marriage that fell apart. And from me, that's for sure. They know a lot of my secrets. They know a lot of my now young-adult kids' secrets. And yet their faces still light up before us. Their love pours out more. The big secret of grace is how my mom and dad attend our events together, with their new, old spouses. And they ask how the other is doing. Oh, Jesus is there. And he's very recognizable.

Of course, there are the particular legacies they each hand down: my dad's resourcefulness and art in combining the strange ingredients left the day before grocery day into a fabulous meal, his ability to see the naked face and listen to his instincts so well, his inability to small talk (which enables deep sharing), and the premeditation he puts into setting up his jokes. He always makes us laugh—or roll our eyes. You can see my mom's legacy in her way of being late but somehow turning it into just in time, the way everything she touches turns gold (things have a way of working out for her), the way she can really listen without interrupting (which makes you feel heard), and how she is always inviting company over yet is never out of food, or the energy to make it. This is such a short list, but I have a word count to tend to. Their generosity oozes out in all the above and in so many other ways. I feel like Mom and Dad when I am exercising any of these traits. Are these not a plethora of ways to see and learn about Jesus as well?

This long and bumpy search of finding a church to belong with has also revealed parts of the face of Jesus that I would not have seen had I remained in my childhood denomination or the Presbyterian denominations we raised our children in. I am receiving a legacy from Christians in denominations I would have discounted before. The nondenominational churches have taught me that we can sit at circular tables if we want, looking at each other's faces instead of the backs of heads. They've taught me the beauty and importance of the priesthood of all believers and seeing the marginalized as people, not projects. Oh, Jesus is so there. The Black church has taught me about the power of witness. And introduced me to the weeping Jesus. Don't we all need to learn more about how to lament well? I still haven't learned about why the Anglicans like those big necklaces, but I have learned more about the symbolism in their vestments. And I really felt in tune with the Spirit and the others praying with me at a compline service. I am learning so much at the Methodist church, about how to rest in the liturgy of the church calendar; how a child can serve me, saying, "This is the body of Christ broken for you," with the Spirit powerfully working; about lay ministers; shorter, pastoral sermons; and so much more. Sure, we expect Jesus to show up in church, but it hasn't been in the prescribed ways I previously thought he'd be revealed.

God keeps showing up in peculiar places. What a joy to discover him over and over. Maybe that is what we can remember most throughout the generations to come, when the shapes of our faces are forgotten. We have something eternal to deposit.

THE LEGACY OF FAITH

Providence is a strange thing. So mysterious. And I don't know how to say this elegantly, so I will just say it. Yesterday I sat in a room with a dead man for almost four hours. It was my father-in-law. I was there, with my hand lying on his shin, watching his face as it breathed his last breath. I saw life leave his face. And prayed for God to take his Spirit. I tried to muster up all the faith I could for this prayer, and I'll tell you why. He was not a man of faith. I journaled about this just before he died.

December 4, 2023

Matt told me that his dad looks haunted in that hospital bed. Like he is looking back on his life with regrets, and now there is nothing he can do about it. He is unable to communicate any of it. And Matt is saying this while being haunted himself with all these decisions he's had to make on behalf of his father's care. I can convince him that there's really nothing else to do. His father's dementia took such a nose dive when he got Covid. He was no longer able to swallow, and his medical directive was clear. But Matt's worried about his dad's faith. That's where he is second-guessing whether he could have done more to show his dad the love of God. We can't force someone to believe or to love. The best I could tell him was that he's shown it to him over and over. He's seen it in our household. We've shared the gospel with him. He even attended church with us when he stayed over. What a sadness to hold, though.

Never seeing his dad rejoice over the joy of forgiveness and the goodness of God. And to see him so haunted in his last days.

The author of Hebrews defines faith like this: "Now faith is the reality of what is hoped for, the proof of what is not seen. For by this our ancestors were approved" (Heb. 11:1–2). We didn't think we could hope for my father-in-law. This ancestor did not leave that legacy. He did not see the reality of hope in the promise. And now what? But then I remembered something that I learned about earlier.[1] Something that left me in wonder. What about the friends of the paralyzed man who brought him to Jesus on a stretcher? "Seeing their faith, Jesus told the paralytic, 'Have courage, son, your sins are forgiven'" (Matt. 9:2). Seeing the faith of the friends, who were in a sense enacting prayer, bringing this man to Jesus, Jesus both forgives his sins and heals him. We get no words from the paralyzed man himself before this happens. Or what about another group of friends who couldn't get their buddy to Jesus to be healed? All those important people were surrounding Jesus. So they think outside the box, and "they went up on the roof and lowered him on the stretcher through the roof tiles into the middle of the crowd before Jesus. *Seeing their faith* he said, 'Friend, your sins are forgiven'" (Luke 5:19–20, emphasis mine).

Do I have that kind of faith for my father-in-law? A man that was so hardened to God and now unable to communicate or comprehend? What do I believe God will do with him?

Lord, I pray for my unbelief. My doubt in your goodness. My presumption to know goodness. Hope lives here. I just don't know what it looks like.

Hope disrupts.

What a picture for us: it is too crowded to get to Jesus. What a metaphor for our own minds and hearts, crowding him out by our legalism, doubt, idealism, unmoored piety, and wanting to manage God or those who may seem like more important Christians. We need friends who hope for us, who think outside of our box to get us to Jesus. And how interesting it is, seeing the faith of their friends, Jesus—the friend of sinners—forgives and heals. Jesus calls the paralyzed man "friend." How beautiful those words must have been! That is why his sins are forgiven—because Jesus is his friend.

Perhaps we could live now as these friends we see in Scripture, provoking prophetic imagination for when we will all come before the face of Jesus. Perhaps then, on that Great Day, we will feel a familiarity, because we haven't sought him on our own—our friends have brought us to him time and time before.

Could my father-in-law recognize Jesus from our friendship? How many times have we brought him before the face of Jesus by our own faces?

He's every bit as helpless to come before you on his own now as those crippled men in the gospels. But he's still alive. He's still loved. Hope resides near our anguish. Can he see what is real, maybe now more than ever? I pray an ancient, bold blessing, Lord. That you would bless my father-in-law. That you would keep him. That you would cause your face to shine upon him. And give him peace.

Seventeen

THE RIDDLE OF THE OWLS

Videos keep popping up on my social media apps, tutorials to disguise my hooded eyes. Yes, I've noticed them too, in the mornings and in pictures where I'm smiling but something looks different. The hooded eye, they call it. It came for me.

The internet wants to help me with this problem. All the influencers are on it. And so are the tips and products they sell.

I can't stop my face from being forty-eight. My hooded eyes rat me out. We are rebranded by the names the beauty industry delineates to our development: crow's feet, sun damage, laugh lines, which are now called parentheses. Apparently, my mouth is now enclosed, nonessential information. What is essential to know is the aging that's happening around it: tarnished, expiring beauty.

Is it the Grim Reaper coming for my eyes—the hood of death? Is he bringing death to the power of beauty, the power of femininity, or even the ability to be seen? Perhaps I will like the discretion the hood provides—the disruption, even, to the raw, alluring power of youth. Maybe wrinkles offer a testimony to the power of my story. It's there on my face.

All the signals that I ignored before are manifesting. The little lines forming around my lips reveal that I am an anxious person. They tattle on me, saying, "Look at this, you chew your lips all the time!" Wow, I never realized it. I always thought of myself as easygoing, and here I am eating my own flesh. I've been nervously consuming myself for years, and now there are grooves in the path my mouth contorts to make it so.

The lines of much laughter are there—enclosing my mouth, framing my eyes, jetting out like fireworks. All the years of laughing. I'm proud of these.

But I didn't expect the underneath. Underneath my mouth reveals lines of criticalness. All the harsh judgment of others. It's there on my face now. Yes, I see those little curves under my mouth. They've crept between my eyebrows too. I see them and I repent.

The burdens I bear have formed dark pillows for my eyes to rest on. They are fluffier in the mornings, giving my eyes time to wake up. I dutifully attempt to conceal them every day. Others do not need to know these dark burdens. They can only be trusted to be seen and held by a few. Of course, you see them anyway, concealed burdens trying to behave themselves.

All the expressions over the years appear on my forehead. I remember people used to tell me that I had a very expressive face. And now it's revealed. I look at women my age with smooth foreheads thinking of all the visages they held in over the years—or possibly injected over.

Perhaps I will try the lid hack offered by these influencers. Perhaps when I do, I will believe that my face will tell a different story, that something as simple as makeup can hide what the face demands.

MY AGING SELF

It seems fitting to end my memory work here looking in the mirror again. Only the hooded eye is a present memory. I wonder what the ten-year-old me with the bad haircut would think if she saw her aging self. What would she think about my face changing? Would she see it how others do? Could she get to my naked face and tell me who I am now? And what do I know? Would she be proud of what is meaningful to me, how I love others, how I testify to Christ, and how I am longing more and more to experience God in the present? Would she like my haircut by a real, swanky hair stylist who is also my daughter?

If I could look in the mirror and see that little girl, how would I answer some of these questions? What would I tell her? I'd tell her to hang onto her *k-nowledge*. I'd pronounce the *k*. She'd get it. My college roommate and I often pronounced the silent *k*. It was a hat tip to the type of degree that college doesn't offer. The one where you learn that absorbing and regurgitating information doesn't make you wise. Curiosity and wonder do. And so you have to ask, Why *is* the *k* silent? You find out, of course. But you are not satisfied. So you decide to give voice to the *k* sometimes to throw people off. You try to make them curious, even if it makes you look stupid. And then you find out if they are in the k-nowledge club.

What I k-new then was important. I'd tell little Aimee that she was going to get too caught up in other matters—that were significant, but made us forget about the *k*. As Duke ethicist Stanley Hauerwas put it, our faith "is not a set of doctrines one believes in order to be a Christian, but rather Christianity is to have one's body shaped, one's habits determined, in such a way that the worship of God is unavoidable."[1] Little Aimee, you're going to need to learn a lot more about God. Some of that involves doctrine and theology. But don't get tangled up into thinking that people with the most right information are the spiritually mature. Don't think doctrinal knowledge measures love or earns more intimate encounters with God. You're going to have to learn this the hard way. The revelation of the lack of spiritual and emotional maturity among church leaders and academics is going to knock you off your feet for a while. When this happens, look at yourself in the mirror and remember this.

And let's talk about intimate encounters with God. You feel that now before you fall asleep at night. The trust you have—that you have to have—before surrendering to unconsciousness. You feel his Spirit with you. And you often talk to him until you fade. You have this trust because of the love of your family. As you grow, God's going to seem silent or distant sometimes. It's because you are losing your sense of listening and looking. He doesn't ever leave you. Barbara Brown Taylor reminds us that God promises to show up in the faces of others. But don't just use people's faces to find God. "Paradoxically, the point is not to see him. The point is to see the person standing right in front of me, who has no substitute, who can never be replaced, whose heart holds things for which there is no language, whose life is an unsolved mystery."[2] Look at the faces of others with the same curiosity with which you look at your face in the mirror. You'll hear a lot of talk about loving your neighbor. You need to learn that this is an investment of your time. You need to look with love. Continue to love people particularly, and you will keep your sense of awe and curiosity. I agree with Taylor that "I am not sure it is possible to see the face of God in other people if you cannot see the faces they already have."[3] Of course, this is hard to do when we are still forming our own faces.

Little Aimee, your face is going to go through some changes. You don't get to see it as others do, and it will be a struggle to stop trying. It's hard enough to see your own face in that reflection in the mirror, to figure out who the *you* is that you're looking at. You'll stop looking underneath your tongue and eyelids and begin to notice wrinkles around them instead. But you will have awesome hair because you will never forget your rattail. And thankfully, you will still take hairstyling risks because you keep your sense of adventure. Your hair will be all the colors and all the lengths, and you will have fun with it all because you're listening to me right now and you won't take yourself too seriously on this.

TELLING OUR SECRETS

Mostly, I want little Aimee to dig up her secrets. We don't think we can look too closely at them. And we certainly cannot speak them. But they keep us stuck. Jesus is hanging out in our secrets, waiting for us. Getting to them is as simple as paying attention to those nagging thoughts and sensations that we try to distract ourselves from and to consider what it is we really want. Children are so good at this because they know how important it is. When they make friends, they want to know about their new companion's favorites and fears. We need to keep asking these questions. What do you love, and what do you fear? What keeps you up at night? What do you want to get out of bed for? And then we need to go deeper. What are your wounds, what makes you anxious, what are you ashamed of, what do you wish you would have said or not said that time, what are your missed opportunities, when have you sabotaged yourself and others? What brings you delight? What makes your heart sing?[4] Telling our stories helps us find our secrets. This kind of looking in the mirror is good life work. Frederick Buechner tells us why: "I am my secrets. And you are your secrets. Our secrets are human secrets, and our trusting each other enough to share them with each other has much to do with the secret of what it is to be human."[5] This is the secret that God is teaching us—what it is to be human.

"THE PORTAL TO THE RICHNESS INSIDE US"

Prayer is a form of secret telling. We can get good practice in with God as we are learning what it is to be human. My journaling is like this. Renita Weems writes about her own prayer journaling and how looking back at how she filled her pages reveals twenty years of being absorbed with the same types of worries and wants. Maybe they seem embarrassing, as if at this point in her life her prayers should be more sophisticated. And yet she writes about the importance of telling her secrets to God and her gratefulness for these "stutters before the holy."

Still, I've learned some things from this long affair with written prayers. For one thing, sometimes you have to pray the prayers you can until you can pray the prayer you want. Second, prayer is not so much learning to write or talk to someone or some presence outside yourself as it is becoming mindful of a conversation already taking place deep inside.[6]

This is some gold. Weems helped me to see my own journaling as stutters before the holy. I've learned to let myself sound stupid. Because ~~sometimes~~ I am, and God already knows it. I am trying to get to the truth, trying to get to that conversation already taking place inside, and to do that, you have to get the other stuff out. Whatever thoughts are tapping me on the shoulder, be it annoyances, fears, to-do lists, unmet desires, or stresses. Then there are all the stupid things we ask for to distract us from the fear of the big things we need to ask for. The ones God has created us to launch into. And the theological questions we try to solve to deceive ourselves into certainty about him. We deceive ourselves into thinking we can manage him or distract ourselves from that ever-looming question about his goodness toward us. We are too busy trying to be good rather than beholding goodness. Think of all the prayers we have to pray until we can pray the prayer we want.

Weems is channeling the medieval contemplative Teresa of Ávila here at the end. That conversation already taking place deep inside, if only we can find it, is what Teresa calls the interior castle, where our Spirit experiences our unity with Christ. And all these prayers we pray to get to the prayers we need to pray are "like the fool who cannot find his assigned seat."[7] The mind is restraining itself and in need of a traffic director.

Journaling helps me find that place or, I should say, get closer to it. My best prayers come out on the page. I don't even know it sometimes until I look back and see all those prayers I had to pray. The pages are full of my thoughts that needed to find their assigned seats and be quiet. There are the prayers I had to pray that help me to shed the faux parts of me. The page pulls them out, with the work of the Spirit. This process awakens me to the presence of God, who understands my stuttering and patiently waits for me to find clarity to get to my true desires. He waits for me to listen quietly to that conversation already taking place deep inside. No wonder Jesus encourages us to pray in private and shut the door.[8] The countless secrets that Jesus holds.

Anne Lamott wrote a moving piece for the *Washington Post* telling some of the secrets she's learned at sixty-nine. Since I'm only forty-eight (and it feels really good to put the *only* in there), she speaks with more authority than I do. But it is right in line with what Weems was writing in her forties and what I am attempting to get at. She titled it, "At 33, I Knew Everything. At 69, I Know Something Much More Important."[9] Lamott begins by sharing how all that's happening in the news is overwhelming her, how many funerals she is about to attend, how her dear friend is dying in the hospital while waiting on a new liver, and how her own body aches just trying to get out of bed and make the drive to visit. She says,

> I don't think I could have borne up under all this 20 years ago when I thought I knew so much about life. That was not nearly as much as I knew at 33, which is when we

know more than we ever will again. But age has given me the ability to hang out without predicting how things will sort out this time (mostly—depending on how I've slept).[10]

Yes, watch out for thirty-three! We thought it was the teenagers who believed they knew everything. They've got nothing on our thirty-three-year-old selves. But then our secrets start leaking out, if we are lucky. (Now that I'm no longer a Presbyterian, I allow myself to use the word *lucky* again. I just rehearse the theology through my mind and maybe shoot a quick prayer to the Lord saying, "What I mean is, 'your sweet providence.'") And we find meaningfulness in deeper places. Over the years, we realize that knowing isn't all it's cracked up to be. It's a terrible hustle. Lamott tells us the secret: "My white-haired husband said on our first date seven years ago that 'I don't know' is the portal to the richness inside us. This insight was one reason I agreed to a second date (along with his beautiful hands)."[11]

Is Lamott's white-haired husband's portal the same as Weems's conversation already taking place inside? When all our thoughts take their assigned seats, when we look back at all those things that were so important to us in our prayers and see their futility, all the prayers that we had to pray to come to the k-nowledge that we do not know, it is *so* freeing! Lamott talks about this not knowing as our new starting point, a posture of patience, peace, and rest. It helps you see differently. When you don't need to know everything, you can chill out. You gain perspective. "Another gift of aging is the precipitous decline in melodrama. Enjoying how unremarkable life is takes practice and time, and then the little things start to shine and delight. Life gets smaller and in its smallness it starts winking at you."[12]

A WINK FROM CUCKOO LAND

But maybe a melodrama can help us appreciate this: *Cloud Cuckoo Land*.[13] The name itself already makes one question its reality. It's a novel by Pulitzer Prize winner Anthony Doerr. In it, Doerr tells a story about a story, one that weaves together the seemingly obscure stories from its readers who range across the world and eight centuries. In one sense, it's a glorification of a fool's journey—a restless shepherd, a "dull-witted muttenheaded lamebrain,"[14] Aethon, who stumbled into a production of Aristophanes's comedy *The Birds*, believing in the paradise land between the heavens and the earth of which they spoke. He sought a wizard to turn him into a bird because birds alone have access there. But instead he becomes a donkey and then a sea bass that gets trapped in a whale. As providence would have it, there's a castaway wizard inside the whale. And he finally gets his wish to be turned into a bird so he can "fly to the city in the clouds where pain never visits and the west wind always blows."[15]

Once he finally makes it to this utopian land, Aethon, who is now a black crow, is met by two gatekeeper owls. To enter, he must solve their riddle to prove that he is really a bird and not a human in disguise. The riddle, one owl explains, seems "simple at first," but "it's actually quite complicated." But the other guardian owl says he has it backward, "No, no, it will seem complicated at first, but it's actually quite simple." Here is the riddle: "He that knows all that Learning ever writ, knows only this."[16] Aethon "traveled all the way to the edge of the earth and beyond"[17] only to be met with a riddle he cannot solve. He is so close to utopia that he can see the honeycakes and smell the cinnamon. Yet he is turned away. Was his whole life's journey for naught? He really was a fool after all. And so he just says, "Nothing." That's what he knows. Turns out, that is the correct answer! "He that knows all that Learning ever writ knows only this—that he knows nothing yet."[18]

Doerr presents this story of Aethon and *Cloud Cuckoo Land,* or the remains of the story, as a rediscovered Greek codex written by the ancient Antonius Diogenes. It's a comedic and outlandish tale to comfort and spark the imagination of his ill niece. One of our characters affected by the story is an amateur classist, translating the codex, filling in missing pieces relevant to both the recovered text and metaphorically to his own life. It is an overwhelming task because the manuscript is "dirty and wormholed, colonized with mold, as though fungal hyphae, time, and water have collaborated to make an erasure poem."[19] And not all the pages are in the right place.

All the characters in this story are learning life lessons that you can never get from a book or a classroom about love, beauty, sacrifice, longing, taking risks, purpose, and living. These lessons are simple at first, but then we complicate them. Or are they complicated at first, and we come to see how simple they are? I don't know. This posture is the portal to the richness inside us, and we cannot learn it by ourselves. The faces of others draw it out. That is another theme in the book—the illusion of seeking refuge in isolation.

Every day holds secrets. The world wants to show us! Whether in fifteenth-century Constantinople, present day Idaho, or on a spaceship in the future, each character affected by this story is realizing that the world wasn't what they thought it was. They couldn't see yet. They think they're in one world, one story, before they come to learn that "sometimes the things we think are lost are only hidden, waiting to be rediscovered."[20] Curiosity, and longing for meaning and connection, will provoke them to take the risks that lead to this discovery. And these risks and discoveries affect the lives of others. Librarians have a star role in the book as well, as they should. They are the facilitators of imagination, the navigators between worlds, the keepers of the story, who whisper, "*Wander around here long enough, dear . . . and you'll discover a secret or two.*"[21]

The funny thing is, after entering utopia, Aethon comes to realize he would rather be human again, a meager shepherd even, in a world where dancing and death reside together, a world where living involves sacrificing—and involves people. And it's the children in the library who figure out that the pages of the codex are out of order, changing where the story ends. Instead, it ends at Aethon's home. For it never would be told if he remained in Cloud Cuckoo Land. They add a line of their own to the end of the story for their play: "The world as it is is enough."[22] There are plenty more secrets to uncover.

December 21, 2023

Nothing. With my father-in-law's death, I am thinking about this cryptic riddle of the owls. At the end of our lives, what knowledge do we really have? Nothing doesn't mean that the truths we've gained don't matter. Nothing doesn't mean that we throw away our confessions about who God is. Nothing isn't meaninglessness. It is a posture that enables us to behold. It's a recognition of our own stuttering before the holy. A portal to awe and wonder. The bewilderment at the seeds we plant that will somehow burst through the soil, new and alive. The glorious things that we don't know. The secrets the world wants to reveal to us. That God is whispering and winking. The world as it is is enough. Until he resurrects us into the one that is to come. He meets us here. And we find beauty in the dancing and are with one another in the agony of the dying. The joy of withness is in both. Every day holds secrets. Nothing is what we give to God as we receive his grace and behold them.

A big secret is that eternal life has already begun. Erasure is another theme in *Cloud Cuckoo Land*. "Erasure is always stalking us, you know?" Doerr highlights the staying power of a story that "has evaded it for so long."[23] I can do the easy thing right here and gospelize this line. Christ followers have the metanarrative, the story where all other stories find their home—all powerfully true and good. Maybe it would make a good sermon. But I can't help but go back to our faces. My hooded eyes that are now warning me of impending erasure. My youth is being erased. Just this week, I saw the face of my father-in-law ever-so-subtly taking his last breath, and I noticed the way he was holding his mouth before it relaxed into death. What a strange change. I guess we are always holding our mouths a certain way—even when we are on a morphine cocktail, unconscious, and dying.

I think of Orual, at the end of her life, realizing she was barefaced in more ways than one. All this time, all this living, and she hasn't developed a face. We don't need death to erase ourselves.

Unlike the riddle of the owls, there isn't a quiz for us to enter eternal life. Theology matters. But we need to k-now why it matters. If we lose our sense of wonder and awe, and if we aren't awakened by the faces before us, how do we expect to experience God? Will we recognize him on that day when we are face-to-face, since we've listened and looked for him in the faces he's made? We won't be answering questions, we will be beholding the face of God. Will his face, like a mirror, show me my own? What will I see?

Lord, that's what this book is: a quest to meditate on your face and the meaningfulness in the faces before us, digging the truth out of ourselves and one another. But it's also an ambiguous "I don't know" as I look back on my life. I'm having to unlearn so much. And the things little Aimee knew about you seem truer. That is what I do know, even if I don't have all the words and the pages in order. The realness of the goodness of you. Your disciples in Scripture constantly stuttered before you. And yet they knew you. They could answer when you asked them. I know their confessions to be true. I see with Martha, that "you are the Messiah, the Son of God, who comes into the world" (John 11:27). Who comes into the world! Which is why this world as it is is enough. Eternal life has already begun. I will wander around here long enough, cracking my shins on altars, looking for secrets.

Eighteen

ANNA, FACE-TO-FACE WITH JESUS

> There was also a prophetess, Anna, a daughter of
> Phanuel, of the tribe of Asher. She was well along
> in years, having lived with her husband seven years
> after her marriage, and was a widow for eighty-
> four years. She did not leave the temple, serving
> God night and day with fasting and prayers. At
> that very moment, she came up and began to
> thank God and to speak about him to all who were
> looking forward to the redemption of Jerusalem.
> —Luke 2:36-38

Daughter of Asher, prophetess through the ages, how fitting
that it is you who sees, you who beholds the face of God,
you who are so very old. And God's face appears in a babe,
forty days old.

You were seven years married. Seven is the number of
completion. God's written Word to us begins and ends in

sevens: seven days of creation, seven churches, seven bowls, seven seals, seven angels. Your seven years of marriage prophesies to us of our own perfect union *to God*.

Luke wants us to know the details about who you are. Such a small cameo in all the New Testament, and most of it is descriptive. What does Luke want us to see? You are mysterious like Melchizedek. Seven years married, eighty-four years widowed.[1] All these numbers trace the history of your people: a virgin betrothed, delivered out of Egypt, and then widowed for so long: eighty-four years. The complete number of seven multiplied by the number of your people, twelve. Elsewhere, the number of leftover baskets of bread.[1] Always on the mind of the Bridegroom, you picture the fullness of God's people.

Eighty-four years widowed. But the story you embody is much older. The echo of your lineage as a daughter of Asher resounds. And we recall the other named daughter from the tribe of Asher—his daughter Serah.[2] It was the daughter of Asher, they say, who assured your people that Moses would redeem Israel from Egypt. Both daughters from the tribe of Asher hold a secret.

What secret do you hold? You reveal the face of God. Anna of Asher, it was always you. Your father's name, Phanuel, means "face of God." His very name is an echo of the place Jacob wrestled with the Lord.[2] He was holding on as best he could until his blessing—the blessing that marked him with a limp. A beautiful, testifying limp. Don't we know it.

---

1. There is some ambiguity in the text as to whether Anna was eighty-four years old or widowed for eighty-four years.

2. Most Bible translations spell it "Serah," but in the majority of rabbinic literature, it is spelled "Serach."

Asher's daughter is before you with the secret. The echoes of her faithfulness are spoken through the ages of Jewish midrash, the ancient oral teaching that carried sparkling truths hidden in its stories.[3] As it is told, the letters of redemption were passed down from patriarch, to patriarch, to patriarch, to patriarch, to daughter. Yes, Abraham, to Isaac, to Joseph, to Jacob and his brothers. And Asher took that promise and delivered it to his daughter, Serah, the keeper of the secret. The assurance that God will take notice—that's the secret. It's the promise of visitation. "And Joseph said to his brethren, 'I am dying; but God will surely visit you, and bring you out of this land to the land of which He swore to Abraham, to Isaac, and to Jacob'" (Gen. 50:24 NKJV). The brothers died. Serah, daughter of Asher, remained with the words of promise, waiting to hear them again and to know.[4]

She is a rabbinic legend, which speaks to the anomaly of her age and the meaning of her name. Serah means "overlapping."[3] She overlaps the generations of Jacob's family descending to Egypt (Gen. 46:17) and the Israelite census in the desert, which takes place hundreds of years later, as the only woman named (Num. 26:46). What breadcrumbs of mystery are left for us in God's Word! How is she this old? Why is a woman named with the sons? How did she not marry or have children? What is the significance of her name and her presence in these historic moments? As the Jewish rabbinic oral tradition tells it, Serah plays key roles in historic turning points of Israel's history. She was the one Joseph's brothers asked to let Jacob know that his son was alive. And for this joy, he gave her a blessing like that of

---

3. Serah's name in extra-biblical texts, Serach, can mean "overhanging, overlapping" (see Ex. 26:12).

Elijah: "Jacob blessed Serach when she spoke these words before him, and he said unto her, my daughter, may death never prevail over thee, for thou hast revived my spirit."[5] She lives on as Lady Wisdom lives on.[6]

When the elders of Israel sought her, telling her about Moses and Aaron and all the signs they performed, Serah was not impressed. But when they said the letters rooted in the sacred words that God told Moses to share with the elders (Ex. 3:16), she knew. These were the letters of visitation. God had taken notice. He was present. These words speak the promise, "God will surely visit you." When Serah heard this, she affirmed the call of Moses. He would redeem Israel out of Egypt because she heard the words from the God who sees, who notices, and who visits. And the people believed (Ex. 4:31) according to the oral teaching of Jewish midrash.[7]

Yes! There's an echo through the ages. And the Lord took notice of his people . . .

Lord, take notice of me.

These words are the letters of redemption. God sees; therefore he moves. That's the secret. The true God takes notice. Serah, the daughter of Asher, was the elder that contained this secret—so they would know that Moses was the one God sent to redeem them.[8] Now it's all coming together. The daughter joins her voice with the Spirit. The woman, created second, is a picture of what is to come: the second order, Zion.

And you are a picture of Zion, Anna. Your name means "full of grace." It's an echo of Hannah, whom God noticed and who poured out her heart and soul in the temple.[9] Like you. And now you too are awaiting a baby.

Anna of Asher, from the northern tribe of Israel, which

has dispersed yet is making its way back to Jerusalem, echo of Serah, you've made your way to the temple where you belong. You are waiting with your secret, waiting to bear witness. The second witness, as the law requires,[10] as creation reveals,[11] whispering the secret of the second order of creation—it's coming. It's breaking in, even now, as the baby boy is presented to the Lord in his temple. Your age, your life, your feminine body, and your heritage testify that redemption of all of Jerusalem is Phanuel, the face of God, in Jesus the Christ, who is the blessed one and one who makes blessed, the true Asher.[12] Jesus is the one who will visit his people and lead them out of slavery, the true Moses. He is the one who hangs on to be blessed by God while stricken, the true Jacob, and the one who strips himself of his glory and travels through the wilderness with his people, whose flesh and bones make it to the promised land, the true Joseph.

Simeon, the first witness in the temple, proclaims that he can now die in peace, recognizing the promise the Holy Spirit revealed to him that he would not see death until his eyes beheld the Lord's Messiah.[13] The old covenant is complete. You, Anna, live on, testifying to all who are looking for the true Bridegroom.

Your dead husband has come back to you, Zion. You no longer sit alone.[14] Your testimony is our testimony. The old gives way to the new and is kissed by the new.[15] The lost tribes return. The fullness of Israel is enfleshed, smiling at her Savior, impregnated with the seed of the whole church. And the church is all who are looking for the face of the true Bridegroom.

We are echoes of you, Anna. Face-to-face, we too begin to see the secret: Jesus. He shows us the face of God. We can see God's face in each other and through the ages. We listen and look. We catch glimpses and we wait—like Anna. As Frederick Buechner so aptly put it: "Wait for him whose face we all of us know because somewhere in the past we have faintly seen it, whose life we all of us thirst for because somewhere in the past we have seen it lived, have maybe even had moments of living it ourselves."[16]

Invitation

LET ME SEE YOUR FACE

How are you telling your story? What conversation is taking place deep inside between you and God? What face is forming?

Here's the paradox: if "I don't know" is our portal to the richness inside of us, we finally have a place to watch our faces develop. Every day, we can choose to lay aside the hustle and be able to wonder at what we discover. *Saving Face* is a triple entendre—maybe it has even more than three meanings. There's the original meaning of the expression. We have this face that we think we are supposed to have, so we are always putting it on, carrying on the hustle it demands, saving face over and over again when we slip out of character. We can continue this striving for our entire lives, like Orual in *Till We Have Faces*. We can even be keeping record, like her, at how wronged we've been and how valiant we are in our decisions and actions, all while keeping a veil over our bareface. Hiding our ugly gives us a feeling of power. But that isn't life-giving (or face-giving) power. As Orual learned, her words and complaints were all jibber-jabber when she was without her veil before the gods. She learned that her whole face was an "I don't know." How can we expect to meet God—or even one another—face-to-face till we have faces?

And so here we are, actually *Saving Face*. We didn't know. We don't know. But we get to call forth our memories, looking for pieces of ourselves in them. We see that little girl or boy that was full of wonder, who suffered humiliation, who harmed others, who had unmet longings. We see that teenager who was trying to make sense of belonging and their social world. These memories that made us stuff parts of our selves down and cover them with a veil. We get to revisit them with curiosity, blessing the desire to be seen and known, naming and lamenting the fractures to our faces. We can share this with trusted others who will witness to not only these stories but also our faces that are forming through them.

By this, we get to help discover one another's faces. All the characters in our lives have faces that beckon our own. We have the opportunity to bless or to curse, to see or neglect, to listen and look for how God is beckoning us in the faces of others, to look for the "here I am" behind the countenances of the face of our neighbor. The things that we don't know about our selves and one another and God get summoned for discovery, if we just uncover the veil.

Mostly, we need *the* Saving Face. God has a face in Jesus Christ. He holds up the mirror for our own faces to emerge. "For now we see only a reflection as in a mirror, but then face to face. Now I know in part, but then I will know fully" (1 Cor. 13:12). We are learning love; our souls are being prepared for love. And we are a part of that love—our distinct faces. Somehow the stories and the secrets that they hold are part of this grand narrative of love.

This is true for us individually as well as corporately in the church. I've experienced so much of that first meaning—a church that is saving face with cover-up, manufactured certainties, clinging to the institution over the people, performative worship, curated programs, and faux belonging. By saving face, the church has lost her face.

Yet there are many amid the disillusionment looking for the face of the church. Can we uncover ourselves from these veils and show our bareface? That's what Scripture does for us, right? It's all there. There are no forced smiles, no tidy bows at the end of the narratives. The history of God's people reveals all the depravity, all the disordered desire, all the loneliness, all the aching, all the disillusionment, intertwined with the wonder and love and glory of God and humanity. The project of saving our faces and coming together in covenantal unity and communion with the triune God and one another—what a sight to behold! What a story to tell!

To see the face of the church in her glory, we need to direct our gaze to the one she beholds: the face that is beckoning hers and that calls her out from hiding to see what is real.

> My dove, in the clefts of the rock,
> in the crevices of the cliff,
> let me see your face,
> let me hear your voice;
> for your voice is sweet,
> and your face is lovely. (Song 2:14)

Invitation

Do you see the invitation? Do you long for it? The true Saving Face beckons the face of his people—all our distinct faces—the faces he is creating in that call. We continue to listen and look for his face in our selves and one another, joining in his summons, our hearts leaping a bit at each little "here I am," until we get to that final beholding—till we have faces that will behold the face of God in Jesus Christ together, at last.

ACKNOWLEDGMENTS

It's funny how I never thought I had an interesting life story to tell. As I dipped a ladle into my memories, I was only making a small bowl and leaving a whole pot of soup on the stove. There is so much more to say about the marvelous people on these pages, and so many transformative people have been left out, people who are helping me form a face, people who reveal different portraits of the face of Christ, and—to mix my metaphors some more—people who make up the roux. They are my thickening agents, who also contribute to my nutty flavor. Listing their names in the acknowledgments section seems too reductive.

Storied memory work is vulnerable. And personal. It's a visitation of how my mind has been holding the memory, what emotions have been clinging to it, examining how that memory has shaped me. It's a looking into my younger face and the faces of those in the memory, asking what needs lamented, what needs blessed, and how I might relook and retell it. Why has this memory stuck the way it has? How might all this reexamining shape my sense of self, relationships, and faith? And of what I know of the divine face? The memories are real as they live in my mind and soul and body. But others in them may hold different versions of the same moments. And so sharing my memories isn't only vulnerable for me but also for the people in them. I hope that I honored my people well. Part of doing that is letting them be human—like me. And recognizing they have their own stories, their own pasts and present longings. Let's all acknowledge this.

I'm grateful for the freedom in belonging that I have with my parents, my husband, and my friends to be able to share the bowl that I dipped out. And I'm thankful for the conversations and love that have come from it. A name or two has been changed in the telling, for privacy.

I'm grateful for my agent, Don Gates, and the Zondervan Reflective team for believing in this project. Thanks to Katya Covrett and Alexis De Weese for helping me rein my abstract, creative writing into a palatable handle for a book. And thanks to both Katya and Matt Estel for the hard work in the editing and copy-editing process, making this manuscript more presentable and this author continue to grow in her craft.

So much of book formation and writing is not done at the desk or on the page. It percolates in conversations. And much of the time, my conversation partners receive a lot of partially formed ideas and thoughts. Beans of inspiration boiling in my head with no direction yet, much of which wants to brew more while I'm hiking with friends. So for my friends who have tasted the ideas in *Saving Face* before they were ready for pouring—Anna Anderson, Dana Tuttle, Aimee DeWeese, and Amber Jones—thank you not only for listening but for thoughtfully engaging while we were doing the same kind of storytelling as we sauntered up and down mountains. Just think of how many stories the Appalachian

Trail alone holds. And how many faces the Potomac River reflects each day.

Lastly, I want to acknowledge and thank the many great writers in my endnotes. You've stirred me. You've inspired me. You've taught me. What an honor to share in this art of thinking, creating, and publishing.

NOTES

Preface

1. "The relation of one face to the other, or seeing the face of the other . . . , means that I approach the other so that his face acquires meaning for me. Then meaningfulness of the face is the command to responsibility." Emmanuel Levinas, *Is It Righteous to Be? Interviews with Emmanuel Levinas*, ed. Jill Robbins (Stanford, CA: Stanford University Press, 2001), 135.

2. See Levinas, *Is It Righteous to Be?*, 108.

Prelude

1. C. S. Lewis, *Till We Have Faces: A Myth Retold* (1956; Orlando: Harcourt Brace, 1984), 291.

2. Lewis, *Till We Have Faces*, 292.

3. Lewis, *Till We Have Faces*, 294.

4. Lewis, *Till We Have Faces*, 308.

5. Some excerpts in this prelude borrow from Aimee Byrd, *The Hope in Our Scars: Finding the Bride of Christ in the Underground of Disillusionment* (Grand Rapids: Zondervan Reflective, 2024), 152–56.

6. Rowan Williams, *Where God Happens: Discovering Christ in One Another* (Boston: New Seeds, 2005), 68.

7. Clare of Assisi, "The Third Letter to Agnes of Prague" (1238), in *Clare of Assisi: The Lady*, trans. and ed. Regis J. Armstrong, Early Documents, rev. ed. (New York: New City, 2006), 51.

Chapter 1: Looking for My Face

1. See Malcolm Guite, "A Grain of Wheat," in *Parable and Paradox: Sonnets on the Sayings of Jesus and Other Poems* (Norwich: Canterbury, 2016).

2. Cole Arthur Riley, *This Here Flesh: Spirituality, Liberation, and the Stories That Make Us* (New York: Convergent, 2023), 81.

3. Curt Thompson, MD, refers to the awful narrating self in *The Soul of Shame: Retelling the Stories We Believe about Ourselves* (Downers Grove, IL: InterVarsity Press, 2015), 58.

4. Adapted from Richard Rohr, *Franciscan Mysticism: I Am That Which I Am Seeking*, disc 3 (Center for Action and Contemplation, 2012), https://cac.org/daily-meditations/the-face-of-the-other-2019-01-31/.

5. Walter Brueggemann, *The Prophetic Imagination*, 40th Anniversary ed. (Minneapolis: Fortress, 2018), 56.

6. See Brueggemann, *Prophetic Imagination*, 56–57.

7. Brueggemann, *Prophetic Imagination*, 57.

8. Brueggemann, *Prophetic Imagination*, 57.

Chapter 2: Past, Present, and Eternal Mirrors

1. Adapted from Richard Rohr, *Franciscan Mysticism: I Am That Which I Am Seeking*, disc 3 (Center for Action and Contemplation, 2012), https://cac.org/daily-meditations/the-face-of-the-other-2019-01-31/.

2. Jim Wilder, *Renovated: God, Dallas Willard, and the Church That Transforms* (Colorado Springs: NavPress, 2020), 36.

3. Clare of Assisi, "The Third Letter to Agnes of Prague" (1238), in *Clare of Assisi: The Lady*, trans. and ed. Regis J. Armstrong, Early Documents, rev. ed. (New York: New City, 2006), 51.

4. *Clare of Assisi*, 55, emphasis original.

5. *Clare of Assisi*, 61.

Chapter 3: What Is Held Inside

1. See Daniel J. Siegel, MD, *Mindsight: The New Science of Personal Transformation* (New York: Bantam, 2010), 59–63. This section borrows significantly from Siegel's work on these pages.

2. Siegel, *Mindsight*, 60.

3. Siegel, *Mindsight*, 62.

4. Siegel, *Mindsight*, 63.

5. "Kayfabe," Wikipedia, accessed July 13, 2023, https://en .wikipedia.org/wiki/Kayfabe.

Chapter 4: What Does the Mirror Reveal?

1. Aimee Byrd, *The Sexual Reformation: Recovering the Dignity and Personhood of Man and Woman* (Grand Rapids: Zondervan Reflective, 2022).

2. Prof. Rabbi Rachel Adelman, "A Copper Laver Made from Women's Mirrors," TheTorah.com, https://www.thetorah .com/article/a-copper-laver-made-from-womens-mirrors.

3. There is much debate about the "ministering" part of this verse. Is the word here, *tzov't*, a Levitical function, as used in Numbers 4:23, 35, 39, 43; and 8:24? Or, a soldier/ military term as in Numbers 31:7; Isaiah 29:7, 8; 31:4;

and Zechariah 14:12? Some commentators suggest these women helped with the sacrifices or served in examining the women who came to worship for ritual purity (as we see the Levitical priests function as gatekeepers in this way in 2 Chronicles 23:19). Susan Ackerman argues this, noting the Vulgate's fourth-century Latin translation of *ha-tzov'ot* as "women who stood guard." She goes as far as to connect these ministering women with the ample ancient Near Eastern archaeological evidence of female figurines, often paired, flanking the entrance to Canaanite and Egyptian shrines. Others suggest the women are only a work force performing menial tasks. (See Adelman, "A Copper Laver Made from Women's Mirrors.")

4. Leland Ryken, James C. Wilhoit, and Tremper Longman III, eds., *Dictionary of Biblical Imagery* (Downers Grove, IL: IVP Academic, 1998), 115.

5. See Byrd, *The Sexual Reformation*, 45–50.

Chapter 5: Disruptions to Our Sense of Self

1. Robert McCloskey, *Centerburg Tales: More Adventures of Homer Price* (Viking, 1951; New York: Puffin, 1977), 165–66.

2. E. F. Schumacher, *A Guide for the Perplexed* (New York: Harper & Row, 1977), 134–35, emphasis in original.

3. Donald Macleod, *From Glory to Golgotha* (Scotland, UK: Christian Focus, 2002), 7, quoted in Aimee Byrd, *No Little Women: Equipping All Women in the Household of God* (Phillipsburg, NJ: P&R, 2016), 117–18.

4. Dallas Willard, *The Divine Conspiracy: Rediscovering Our Hidden Life in God* (London: Collins, 1998), 300.

5. See Makoto Fujimura, *Culture Care* (Downers Grove, IL: InterVarsity Press, 2017), 49, 54.

6. D. C. Schindler, *Love and the Postmodern Predicament: Rediscovering the Real in Beauty, Goodness, and Truth* (Eugene, OR: Cascade, 2018), 81, emphasis original.

Chapter 6: A Good Name

1. Ellen F. Davis, *Proverbs, Ecclesiastes, and the Song of Songs* (Louisville: Westminster John Knox, 2000), 174.
2. Davis, *Ecclesiastes*, 159.
3. See Daniel J. Siegel, MD, *Mindsight: The New Science of Personal Transformation* (New York: Bantam, 2011), 171.
4. Bessel Van Der Kolk, MD, *The Body Keeps the Score: Brain, Mind, and Body in the Healing of Trauma* (New York: Penguin, 2014).

Chapter 7: Communing with Eternity

1. Esther Meek talks about communing with the real in Esther Meek, *Doorway to Artistry: Attuning Your Philosophy to Enhance Your Creativity* (Eugene, OR: Cascade, 2023), 18.
2. Barbara Brown Taylor, *An Altar in the World: A Geography of Faith* (New York: HarperOne, 2009), 15.
3. See also Aimee Byrd, *Why Can't We Be Friends? Avoidance Is Not Purity* (Phillipsburg, NJ: P&R, 2018), 52–56.
4. Abraham Joshua Heschel, *God in Search of Man: A Philosophy of Judaism* (New York: Farrar, Straus and Giroux, 1976), 174.

Chapter 8: The Gaze That Does Us In

1. Luke 22:14–62.
2. Luke 22:28.
3. John 15:15.
4. Luke 22:45–46.
5. John 6:68.

6. Matt. 10:1–2; Mark 3:14–16; 6:7; Luke 6:13; 9:1.
7. John 1:42.
8. Matt. 17:1–16; Mark 9:2–7; Luke 9:28–35.
9. Luke 24:1–12; John 20:1–10.
10. Luke 24:36–49; John 20:19–23.
11. John 21:5.
12. John 21:1–19.

Chapter 9: God Showed Us His Face
1. Gen. 1:4, 10, 12, 18, 21, 22, 25, 27, 31.
2. Matt. 17:1–8; Mark 9:2–8; Luke 9:28–36.
3. Rev. 1:16.
4. Heb. 1:3.
5. This is the title of Amazon Studio's most downloaded documentary limited series, *Shiny Happy People: Duggar Family Secrets*.
6. Caryll Houselander, *The Risen Christ: The Forty Days after the Resurrection* (New York: Sheed & Ward, 1958; repr., Strongsville, OH: Scepter, 2021), 7–8.
7. Houselander, *The Risen Christ*, 8–9.

Chapter 10: Provocations to Blessing
1. Emmanuel Levinas, *Is It Righteous to Be? Interviews with Emmanuel Levinas*, ed. Jill Robbins (Stanford, CA: Stanford University Press: 2001), 211.
2. Levinas, *Is It Righteous to Be?*, 211.
3. Levinas, *Is It Righteous to Be?*, 191.
4. Levinas, *Is It Righteous to Be?*, 106.
5. Levinas, *Is It Righteous to Be?*, 66.
6. Levinas, *Is It Righteous to Be?*, 236.
7. Kate Bowler and Jessica Richie, *The Lives We Actually*

Have: 100 Blessings for Imperfect Days (New York: Convergent, 2023), xvii.

8. Bowler and Richie, *Lives We Actually Have*, xix.

9. Bowler and Richie, *Lives We Actually Have*, xix.

10. Jim Wilder, *Renovated: God, Dallas Willard, and the Church That Transforms* (Colorado Springs: NavPress, 2020), 98.

11. Levinas, *Is It Righteous to Be?*, 170.

Chapter 11: Facing God's Face

1. This is modified from a sermon I gave at Christ Fellowship Church and Central West End Church in Saint Louis, Illinois.

2. Song 2:7; 3:5; 8:4.

3. Gen. 8:10–11; Matt. 3:16.

4. See Aimee Byrd, *The Sexual Reformation: Restoring the Dignity and Personhood of Man and Woman* (Grand Rapids: Zondervan Reflective, 2022), 154.

5. Song 4:8, 15; 5:15; 7:4.

6. Christopher Mitchell, *The Song of Songs*, Concordia Commentary (Saint Louis: Concordia, 2003), 711.

7. Malcolm Guite, "The Annunciation," in *Sounding the Seasons* is © Malcolm Guite, 2012. Published by Canterbury Press.

8. Gregory of Nyssa, *Gregory of Nyssa: Homilies on the Song of Songs*, trans. Richard A. Norris Jr., ed. Brian E. Daley and John T. Fitzgerald (Atlanta: Society of Biblical Literature, 2012), 51, and Norris's footnote, "I.e., the Bride, who in Gregory's exegesis of the Song regularly appears in the role of a mistress to her apprentices."

9. Esther Meek on "Art and Knowing with Esther Meek," *Two Cities* podcast, episode 61, March 24, 2021, https://

podcasts.apple.com/us/podcast/episode-61-art-knowing
-with-dr-esther-meek/id1502131405?i=1000514203917.

Chapter 12: Looking for Marks of His Glory in One Another

1. Grace Hamman, *Jesus through Medieval Eyes* (Grand Rapids: Zondervan Reflective, 2023), 160.

2. Emmanuel Levinas refers to it as the nudity of the face in *Is It Righteous to Be? Interviews with Emmanuel Levinas*, ed. Jill Robbins (Stanford, CA: Stanford University Press: 2001), e.g., 108, 215.

3. Richard Rohr, "Pentecost Sunday: The Divine Sparkplug," *Homilies with Richard Rohr*, Center for Action and Contemplation, May 15, 2016, https://cac.org/podcasts /pentecost-sunday-divine-sparkplug/.

4. See Levinas, *Is It Righteous to Be?*, 49.

5. Levinas, *Is It Righteous to Be?*, 215.

6. Walter Hooper, *C. S. Lewis: A Companion and Guide* (San Francisco: HarperSanFrancisco, 1996), 252.

7. C. S. Lewis, *Till We Have Faces: A Myth Retold* (1956; Orlando, FL: Harcourt Brace, 1984), 294.

8. Hooper, *Companion*, 252, emphasis original.

9. Julia Cameron, *The Artist's Way: A Spiritual Path to Higher Creativity*, 30th anniversary ed. (New York: TarcherParigee, 1992, 2002, 2016), 67.

10. Lewis, *Till We Have Faces*, 308.

11. Howard Thurman, *The Creative Encounter: An Interpretation of Religion and the Social Witness* (Richmond, IN: Friends United Press, 1972), 23–24.

12. Gerard Manley Hopkins, "As Kingfishers Catch Fire," in *Poems by Gerard Manley Hopkins*, ed. Robert Bridges (London: Humphrey Milford, 1918), 54.

Chapter 13: What the Face Demands

1. See Emmanuel Levinas, *Is It Righteous to Be? Interviews with Emmanuel Levinas*, ed. Jill Robbins (Stanford, CA: Stanford University Press: 2001), 215.
2. Levinas, *Is It Righteous to Be?*, 215.
3. Levinas, *Is It Righteous to Be?*, 215.

Chapter 14: Discovering the Death of the Other

1. See Peter A. Levine, PhD, Ergos Institute of Somatic Education, https://www.somaticexperiencing.com/about -peter/.
2. See Aimee Byrd, *The Hope in Our Scars: Finding the Bride of Christ in the Underground of Disillusionment* (Grand Rapids: Zondervan Reflective, 2024), for further discussion on the underground as a powerful liminal space where Christ works by his Spirit.
3. Emmanuel Levinas, *Is It Righteous to Be? Interviews with Emmanuel Levinas*, ed. Jill Robbins (Stanford, CA: Stanford University Press: 2001), 108.
4. Renita J. Weems, *Listening for God: A Minister's Journey through Silence and Doubt* (New York: Simon & Schuster, 1999), 37.

Chapter 15: He Can't Look at Her Face

1. Phyllis Trible, *Texts of Terror: Literary-Feminist Readings of Biblical Narrative*, 40th anniversary ed. (Minneapolis: Fortress, 2022), 80–81.
2. Trible, *Texts of Terror*, 81–82.
3. Trible, *Texts of Terror*, 83.
4. See Trible, *Texts of Terror*, 84–85. Trible also points out that the editor of Judges, along with the prophets and other

allusions in Scripture, also direct our heart to the woman here.

5. "Greater love hath no man than this" (John 15:13 KJV).

Chapter 16: The Legacy of Our Faces

1. See A. J. Swoboda, *After Doubt: How to Question Your Faith without Losing It* (Grand Rapids: Brazos, 2021), 89.

Chapter 17: The Riddle of the Owls

1. Stanley Hauerwas, "The Sanctified Body," in *Embodied Holiness*, ed. Samuel M. Powell and Michael E. Lodahl (Downers Grove, IL: Intervarsity Press, 1999), 22.

2. Barbara Brown Taylor, *An Altar in the World: A Geography of Faith* (New York: HarperCollins, 2009), 102.

3. Taylor, *An Altar*, 103.

4. Some of these questions are adapted from Frederick Buechner, *Telling Secrets: A Memoir* (San Francisco: HarperSanFrancisco, 1991), 38.

5. Buechner, *Telling Secrets*, 39.

6. Renita J. Weems, *Listening for God: A Minister's Journey through Silence and Doubt* (New York: Touchstone, 1999), 62.

7. St. Teresa of Ávila, *The Interior Castle*, trans. Mirabai Starr (New York: Riverhead, 2003), 108.

8. Matt. 6:6–7.

9. Anne Lamott, "At 33, I Knew Everything. At 69, I Know Something Much More Important," *Washington Post*, opinion, November 20, 2023, https://www.washingtonpost.com/opinions/2023/11/20/aging-acceptance-wisdom-albert-bierstadt/.

10. Lamott, "At 33."

11. Lamott, "At 33."

12. Lamott, "At 33."
13. Anthony Doerr, *Cloud Cuckoo Land* (New York: Scribner, 2021).
14. Doerr, *Cuckoo*, 29.
15. Doerr, *Cuckoo*, 325.
16. Doerr, *Cuckoo*, 440.
17. Doerr, *Cuckoo*, 491.
18. Doerr, *Cuckoo*, 445.
19. Doerr, *Cuckoo*, 474.
20. Doerr, *Cuckoo*, 474.
21. Doerr, *Cuckoo*, 496, emphasis original.
22. Doerr, *Cuckoo*, 568.
23. Doerr, *Cuckoo*, 490.

Chapter 18: Anna, Face-to-Face with Jesus

1. John 6:13.
2. Gen. 32:22–32.
3. For helpful articles summarizing midrash on Serach see Moshe Reiss, "Sarah Bat Asher in Rabbinic Literature," Jewish Bible Quarterly, https://jbqnew.jewishbible.org/assets/Uploads/421/JBQ_421_8_reissserach.pdf; Rabbi Yossef Carmel, "Growing Wiser with Age," Beit Midrash, Yeshiva: The Torah World Gateway (website), 7 Tevet 5766, https://www.yeshiva.co/midrash/4222; Tamar Kadari, "Sarah, daughter of Asher: Midrash and Aggadah," The Shelve/Hyman Encyclopedia of Jewish Women, Jewish Women's Archive (website), https://jwa.org/encyclopedia/article/serah-daughter-of-asher-midrash-and-aggadah.
4. See Pirkei DeRabbi Eliezer 48:17. Also see Exodus Rabbah 5:13–14; Shemot Rabbah 5.
5. Sefer ha-Yashar (The Book of Jasher) 54:98.
6. According to midrash, Serach was also the wise woman in

2 Samuel 20:16–22 who stopped Joab from seizing her city by getting the people there to deliver the head of Sheba over the city wall to him. See Bereishit Rabba 94.

7. See Pirkei DeRabbi Eliezer 48:17. Also see Exodus Rabbah 5:13–14; Shemot Rabbah 5.

8. According to midrash, Serach, the daughter of Asher, also reveals to Moses where Jacob's bones are so they can fulfill his dying request for his bones to go with them out of Egypt into the promised land, because God noticed (see Mekhilta d'Rashbi chapter 13 and Tosefta Sotah 4:7).

9. 1 Sam. 1:15.

10. Deut. 17:6; 19:15.

11. Gen. 2:22.

12. Asher means "blessed." Gen. 30:13; Luke 1:48–49.

13. Luke 2:26, 29.

14. Lam. 1:1.

15. Song 1:2.

16. Frederick Buechner, "A Room Called Remember," in *Secrets in the Dark: A Life in Sermons* (San Francisco: HarperSanFrancisco, 2006), 64.

ABOUT THE AUTHOR

Aimee Byrd is writer, speaker, blogger, podcaster, and former coffee shop owner. Aimee is the author of several books, including *The Hope in Our Scars*, *Recovering from Biblical Manhood and Womanhood*, and *The Sexual Reformation*. Her articles have appeared in *First Things*, *Table Talk*, *Modern Reformation*, *By Faith*, *New Horizons*, *Ordained Servant*, *Harvest USA*, and *Credo Magazine*, and she has been interviewed and quoted in *Christianity Today* and *The Atlantic*. Subscribe to Aimee's substack, *Byrd in Your Box*, for more of her writing: aimeebyrd.substack.com.

The Hope in Our Scars

Finding the Bride of
Christ in the Underground
of Disillusionment

Aimee Byrd

Want to Dig Deeper into Handling
Disillusionment with the Church?

Aimee Byrd peels back the church's underlying and pervasive theology of power to face the shame that lurks there and find the lasting hope of belonging in Christ. This book is written to those who have been wounded by the church. To those who have suffered abuse at the hands of church leaders and are left with deep scars. To those who are disillusioned or deconstructing their faith, *The Hope in Our Scars* offers a way forward with a God who walks with us in our affliction and wants to make it into something beautiful.

ZONDERVAN
REFLECTIVE